Japanese

for

Young English Speakers

Volume II
Student Workbook

John Young and Yuriko Uchiyama Rollins
assisted by Melanie K. Bush

Georgetown University Press
Washington, D.C.

Georgetown University Press, Washington, D.C. 20007
© 1997 by Gakko Hojin Kawaijuku, All rights reserved.
Printed in the United States of America
9 8 7 6 5 4 3 2 1
THIS VOLUME IS PRINTED ON ACID-FREE OFFSET BOOK PAPER

ISBN 0-87840-352-3

CONTENTS

INTRODUCTION

(A) How to Write Your Name in Japanese

As you can probably see from the writing on your name card, some characters are written larger than others. The written size of a character directly affects the way a word is pronounced. These effects will be discussed in greater detail later.

For now, you need to notice that the smaller characters are written as one-fourth (1/4) the size of regularly written characters. In order to practice writing your name with characters of correct size, you will first write your name in the row of boxes below. The smaller characters, though, will use only one of the small boxes. The bar used for long vowel sounds takes a full- size box (four small boxes).

After you have written your name once, ask the teacher to approve it.
Once your teacher aproves your writing, try to write your name in smaller size three more times on the lines below.

_____   _____
(first name)   (last name)

_____   _____
(first name)   (last name)

_____   _____
(first name)   (last name)

1

(B) Basic Katakana

Let's find *katakana* that are used in your name.

ア a	イ i	ウ u	エ e	オ o
カ ka	キ ki	ク ku	ケ ke	コ ko
サ sa	シ shi	ス su	セ se	ソ so
タ ta	チ chi	ツ tsu	テ te	ト to
ナ na	ニ ni	ヌ nu	ネ ne	ノ no
ハ ha	ヒ hi	フ hu	ヘ he	ホ ho
マ ma	ミ mi	ム mu	メ me	モ mo
ヤ ya	(イ)* i	ユ yu	(エ)* e	ヨ yo
ラ ra	リ ri	ル ru	レ re	ロ ro
ワ wa	(ヰ)* i	(ウ)* u	(ヱ)* e	ヲ o
ン n'				

shi sounds like "she," *chi* sounds like "<u>chi</u>li," *tsu* sounds like "two ca<u>ts</u>."
* *Katakana* in parentheses indicates that either it is not in current use or it is identical with *a gyoo* symbol both in shape and in pronunciation.

2

(C) Date and Name Box

As you might have guessed, the box at the top right of most pages is for you to write in your name, the date, the day, and your student number. It looks like this:

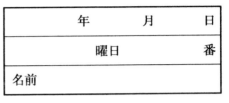

(name sample)

These are new vocabulary words for you to remember:

- 年 *nen* (year)
- 日 *nichi* (day of month)
- 番 *ban* (number) = student number

- 月 *gatsu* (month)
- 曜日 *yoobi* (day of week)
- 名前 *namae* (name)

So that your teacher can maintain records efficiently and correctly, it is important for you to fill in the box whenever you receive handouts.

(D) Mnemonic Device for Learning the order of the Japanese Consonants

In order to memorize the order of the Japanese "50-on," you can make a sentence by applying the mnemonic system.

Examples:

a	all	**a**	all
k	kids	**k**	key
s	say	**s**	students
t	trendy	**t**	take
n	new	**n**	note of
h	hair-styles	**h**	handsome
m	make	**m**	man
y	you	**y**	you
r	really	**r**	really
w	weird	**w**	want
n'	now	**n'**	now

3

Now it is your turn to come up with examples:

a	**a**
k	**k**
s	**s**
t	**t**
n	**n**
h	**h**
m	**m**
y	**y**
r	**r**
w	**w**
n'	**n'**

(E) *Aisatsu* (Exchanging Greetings)

Traditionally, when meeting someone in formal situations, the Japanese people always exchang
bows (*ojigi*). The bow is used to show respect. It accompanies the following actions:

- greeting someone
- expressing appreciation
- making requests

- saying farewell
- making apologies

Points of Information

- For those who want to make a perfect *ojigi*, bend from the waist at a 45° angle. Don'
change the angle of your head (relative to your body) or direction of your eyesight (yo
should be looking directly downward, about three feet in front of you). The legs are kep
straight, and the heels should be together. A man's arms are held close to his sides (not i
his pockets); a woman brings her hands together in front to lightly touch each other.

- The person who is younger/lower in social status or junior in a business relationship, etc., hold
the bow lower and longer than the older/higher- ranking person.

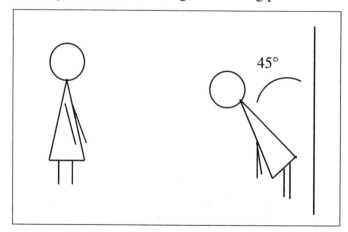

- Nowadays, more and more Japanese use the handshake, especially when meeting Westerners. Some people use the bow and handshake together.

- If you are not sure whether to bow or shake hands with a Japanese person, the best thing to do is simply wait for the other person and be ready to do as he/she does. If the other person makes no move, he/she is probably watching to see what to do, too! In that case, you can take the initiative. If you do not want to bow, nodding with a smile will do.

(F) *"Hajimemashite"* (How do you do)

When you introduce yourself in Japan, your title, such as Dr., Mr., Mrs., Ms., or Miss, is <u>not</u> used. Instead the Japanese say the name of the company you represent or the area of the country you live in as a way of giving further identification.

      Example: • Taroo Honda from Toyota Co.
                         Toyota no Honda Taroo desu.
                  • John Smith from California
                         Kariforunia no Jon Sumisu desu.

When Japanese introduce themselves in Japanese, the last name (family name) goes first and the first name (given name) goes last.

      Example: • Emiko Suyama
                         Suyama Emiko
                  • Isao Matsueda
                         Matsueda Isao

It is normally understood in the Japanese culture that names from non-Japanese cultures should be kept as they would be in their country of origin.

      Example: Charlie Brown

When you address someone by name in Japanese, however, it is essential to add the title or Mr., Mrs., etc.

Forms of Address	Family Name	First Name
- *san*	√	√
- *kun*	√	√
- *chan*		√
- *sensei*	√	√
- *daitooryoo*	√	
- *sama*	√	√

1. **-san** can be used on any occasion with any gender, age, and rank to show respect. (Mr., Ms., Mrs., etc.)

2. **-kun** can be used to address a male (equal or lower status).

3. **-chan** can be used when talking to a little girl or boy. Sometimes people who have grown up together since childhood use the term "*chan*" to show friendship and/or intimacy.

4. **-sensei** is used to show respect to professional people such as lawyers and university professors. Teachers and instructors are included in this rank in Japan.

5. **-daitooryoo** means president of a country. A president of a business or company is called "*shachoo*." A president of an organization/association is called "*kaichoo*."

6. **-sama** was commonly used in the past for members of the aristocratic society. Today, it is sometimes used on written documents or letters when they are very formal.

Exercise:

Choose the best name suffix for the following situations and write the answer in the blank.

_____	Yuriko Rollins, your Japanese language teacher
_____	Yumiko Toyota, Japanese three-year-old girl
_____	Masahiro Wakatsuki, salesperson
_____	Tami Nakamura, your classmate
_____	Nobutaka Takashima, your dentist
_____	Ken Honda, paper boy
_____	Chieko Hattori, a 16-year-old babysitter
_____	Noriko Dan, your friend's mother
_____	George Washington, president of the U.S.A.
_____	When a department store salesperson addresses to his/her customer.

a. *chan*	b. *san*	c. *sama*	d. *kun*	e. *sensei*
f. *daitooryoo*				

nen	gatsu	nichi
	yoobi	ban
namae		

A) In the blanks, write the letter of the English equivalent for each Japanese word. The first 8 words are from Lesson 1; the others are from Volume One.

_____	1.	natsukashii	なつかしい	a.	young
_____	2.	tegami	てがみ	b.	all right
_____	3.	doofuu suru	どうふうする	c.	mountain
_____	4.	natsu	なつ	d.	pictures
_____	5.	shashin	しゃしん	e.	friend
_____	6.	jisaboke	じさぼけ	f.	long for
_____	7.	zuibun	ずいぶん	g.	jet lag
_____	8.	owaru	おわる	h.	stomach
_____	9.	yama	やま	i.	good at
_____	10.	onaka	おなか	j.	box
_____	11.	kookoosei	こうこうせい	k.	extremely
_____	12.	amai	あまい	l.	enclose
_____	13.	hako	はこ	m.	every day
_____	14.	wakai	わかい	n.	summer
_____	15.	sakana	さかな	o.	high school student
_____	16.	joozu	じょうず	p.	voice
_____	17.	daijoobu	だいじょうぶ	q.	letter
_____	18.	koe	こえ	r.	to end
_____	19.	mainichi	まいにち	s.	fish
_____	20.	tomodachi	ともだち	t.	sweet

LESSON 1

nen	gatsu	nichi
	yoobi	ban
namae		

(B) Fill in the blanks of the following conversations with appropriate words or phrases to complete each dialogue. In the parenthesis, write the letter from the list of situations below that best describes each dialogue.

1. (　　) A: *Ojisan, osewa ni narimashita. Korede shitsurei shimasu.*

　　　　B: *Ken chan, kyoo wa yoku kite kureta ne.*

　　　　A: *Ironna hanashi ga kikete totemo tanoshikatta desu.*

　　　　B: *Sore wa yokatta. Kuruma ni wa _____ kaerinasai yo.*

　　　　A: *Hai. Arigatoo gozaimashita. _____.*

　　　　B: *Sayoonara.*

2. (　　) A: *Senjitsu wa kodomo ga taihen _____ ni nari, arigatoo gozaimashita.*

　　　　B: *Iie. Kochira koso. Uchi no Takashi mo itsumo ojama shite iru yoo de sumimasen.*

3. (　　) A: *Honkon e itta toki wa taihen osewa ni narimashita.*

　　　　B: *Iya, kochira koso iroiro arigatoo gozaimashita.*

　　　　A: *Kondo mo issho ni Amerika _____ mitai desu ne.*

4. (　　) A: *Sensei, 4nenkan taihen osewa ni narimashita.*

　　　　B: *Nihongo no benkyoo saigo made yoku ganbatta ne.*

　　　　A: *Sensei no _____ desu. Arigatoo gozaimashita.*

5. (　　) A: *Iroiro osewa ni narimashita. Asu kara tatami no ue de nerarenai no ga zannen desu.*

　　　　B: *Jimu san Nihon ga totemo ki ni itta mitai ne. Watashi mo itsuka Amerika ni itte mitai wa.*

　　　　A: *Ee, zehi _____. Daikangei* (welcome) *shimasu.*

---

a. a student who is about to graduate	d. last day with a homestay family
b. people who traveled abroad together	e. conversation between two mothers
c. a student who visited his uncle	

8

	nen	gatsu	nichi
		yoobi	ban
namae			

C) Fill in the blanks with the correct phrase from the box below. Then answer the questions. Try to think of creative answers.

1. *Warui seiseki* (grade) *o* (   ) *doo shimasu ka?*
   わるいせいせきを （   ） どうしますか。

   _____

2. *Omoi byooki ni* (   ) *doo shimasu ka?*
   おもいびょうきに （   ） どうしますか。

   _____

3. *Okozukai* (pocket money) *ga* (   ) *doo shimasu ka?*
   おこずかいが （   ） どうしますか。

   _____

4. *Michi de kuruma ga* (   ) *doo shimasu ka?*
   みちで くるまが （   ） どうしますか。

   _____

5. *Resutoran de ryoori ga zenbu* (   ) *doo shimasu ka?*
   レストランで りょうりが ぜんぶ （   ） どうしますか。

   _____

6. *Jugyoochuu ni* (   ) *doo shimasu ka?*
   じゅぎょうちゅうに （   ） どうしますか。

   _____

kakatta toki wa かかった ときは	*nemukunatta toki wa* ねむくなった ときは
koshoo shita toki wa こしょうした ときは	*taberarenakatta toki wa* たべられなかった ときは
nakunatta toki wa なくなった ときは	*totta toki wa* とった ときは

LESSON 1

nen	gatsu	nichi
	yoobi	ban
namae		

(D) Match the phrases on the left with the phrase on the right that best completes each sentenc
and fill in the parenthesis with the correct letter. Each phrase on the right is used one tim
only.

1. *Haru ga owatte* (   )
   はるが　おわって（　　）

2. *Bijinesu de seikoo* (success) *shite* (   )
   ビジネスで　せいこうして（　　）

3. *Heya no denki ga kirete* (   )
   へやのでんきが　きれて（　　）

4. *Sengetsu no 23nichi de* (   )
   せんげつの２３にちで（　　）

5. *Kodomo no toki kara no yume datta* (   )
   こどものときからの　ゆめだった（　　）

6. *Nihon kara kaette* (   )
   にほんから　かえって（　　）

7. *Yakyuusenshu o yamete* (   )
   やきゅうせんしゅを　やめて（　　）

8. *Hatarakisugite* (   )
   はたらきすぎて（　　）

9. *Taifuu ga chikazuite* (   )
   たいふうが　ちかずいて（　　）

10. *Minna ni erabarete* (   )
    みんなに　えらばれて（　　）

a. *jisaboke ni narimashita.*
   じさぼけに　なりました。

b. *17sai ni narimashita.*
   １７さいに　なりました。

c. *seitokaichoo ni narimashita.*
   せいとかいちょうに　なりました。

d. *okanemochi ni narimashita.*
   おかねもちに　なりました。

e. *ame ni narimashita.*
   あめに　なりました。

f. *byooki ni narimashita.*
   びょうきに　なりました。

g. *koochi ni narimashita.*
   コーチに　なりました。

h. *natsu ni narimashita.*
   なつに　なりました。

i. *uchuuhikooshi* (astronaut) *ni narimashita*
   うちゅうひこうしに　なりました。

j. *makkura ni narimashita.*
   まっくらに　なりました。

10

年		月		日
	曜日			番
名前				

A) Find and circle the Japanese equivalent of the 12 English words from Lesson 2 listed below. They are written horizontally, vertically, diagonally, and backwards.

O	F	H	G	U	A	I	N	S	B
I	N	A	K	O	O	K	E	K	U
K	U	D	P	Z	O	H	E	I	R
O	A	E	M	J	R	O	S	E	I
D	M	O	T	O	O	S	A	N	I
I	K	I	M	O	E	E	N	U	H
K	E	M	Y	D	Z	N	I	B	S
O	H	N	I	A	U	S	N	I	E
T	J	U	S	N	G	U	P	J	R
D	O	K	U	T	T	E	E	K	U

1. father
2. sometimes
3. showy

4. oneself
5. folding fan
6. happy

7. joke
8. fit
9. elder sister

10. souvenir
11. exchange
12. send

(B) Choose a verb from the box below to fill in the blanks of the following sentences. Verb should be conjugated into the *-oo* form, following the example. Each verb is used only one time.

Example: *Tsukarete kita kara, koko de sukoshi (yasumoo).*
つかれて きたから、ここで すこし（ やすもう ）.

1. *Kono mondai wa boku ni mo wakaranai kara, sensei ni shitsumon (　　　　).*
このもんだいは ぼくにも わからないから、せんせいに しつもん(　　　).

2. *A, moo 11ji han da. Ashita mo asa ga hayai kara, moo (　　　　).*
あ、もう １１じはんだ。あしたも あさが はやいから、もう(　　　).

3. *Rokku myuujikku no shiidii o katte kita kara, minna de (　　　　).*
ロックミュージックの シーディーを かってきたから、みんなで(　　　).

4. *Atsukunatte kita kara, mado o (　　　　).*
あつくなってきたから、まどを(　　　).

5. *Kondo no eiga wa omoshiroi to itte iru kara, tsugi no shuumatsu ni mi ni (*
こんどのえいがは おもしろい といっているから、つぎのしゅうまつに みに(　　　).

6. *Nani mo suru koto ga nai kara, terebi demo (　　　　).*
なにもすることがないから、テレビでも(　　　).

7. *Menbaa ga zen'in kita kara, kaigi o (　　　　).*
メンバーが ぜんいんきたから、かいぎを(　　　).

8. *Koobe made wa tooi kara, shinkansen ni (　　　　).*
こうべまでは とおいから、しんかんせんに(　　　).

9. *Onaka ga suita kara, nani ka (　　　　).*
おなかがすいたから、なにか(　　　).

10. *Choodo 3tsu aru kara, 3nin de (　　　　).*
ちょうど ３つあるから、３にんで(　　　).

akeru あける	*hajimeru* はじめる	*iku* いく	*kiku* きく
miru みる	*neru* ねる	*noru* のる	*suru* する
taberu たべる	*wakeru* わける	*yasumu* やすむ	

12

(C) Translate the following Japanese sentences into English.

1. *Watashi ga ki ni itte iru sukaato wa kore desu.*
   わたしが　きにいっている　スカートは　これです。

   _____

2. *Asoko de mizu o nonde iru uma wa, kotoshi no yuushooba* (winning horse) *desu.*
   あそこで　みずを　のんでいる　うまは、ことしの　ゆうしょうば　です。

   _____

3. *Se ga takakute megane o kakete iru otoko no hito ga, watashi no ojisan desu.*
   せが　たかくて　めがねを　かけている　おとこの　ひとが、わたしの　おじさん　です。

   _____

4. *Hiroshi wa natsuyasumi ga hajimatte kara, ichinichijuu terebi o mite imasu.*
   ひろしは　なつやすみが　はじまってから、いちにちじゅう　テレビを　みています。

   _____

5. *Hon o yoku yonde iru hito wa, joozu na bun o kaku koto ga dekimasu.*
   ほんを　よく　よんでいる　ひとは、じょうずな　ぶんを　かくことが　できます。

   _____

6. *Watashi ga namae o shitte iru supootsu senshu wa, 5nin shika imasen.*
   わたしが　なまえを　しっている　スポーツせんしゅは、5にん　しか　いません。

   _____

7. *Tonari no teeburu de nigirizushi o tabete iru obasan wa, namida* (tears) *o nagashite imasu.*
   となりの　テーブルで　にぎりずしを　たべている　おばさんは、なみだを　ながしています。

   _____

8. *Nyuu Yooku Yankiisu no booshi o kabutte iru ano hito wa, igirisujin desu.*
   ニューヨークヤンキースの　ぼうしを　かぶっている　あのひとは、イギリスじんです。

   _____

9. *Ima anata ga yonde iru hon wa nan desu ka?*
   いま　あなたが　よんでいる　ほんは　なんですか。

   _____

10. *Inu to asonde iru kodomo wa, watashi no itoko desu.*
    いぬと　あそんでいる　こどもは、わたしの　いとこです。

    _____

LESSON 3

(A) Fill in the blank spaces of the following verb conjugation chart. The verbs are from Lessons 1 and 2 as well as from Volume One.

#	Dictionary Form	Pre -*masu* + -*masu*	-*oo* Form	English: Pre -*masu* + -*masu*
1	arau			
2				blow
3			hanasoo	
4			ikoo	
5		iimasu		
6	kaesu			
7		kakimasu		
8				buy
9				cut
10		machimasu		
11			miseyoo	
12	nomu			
13		okurimasu		
14			owaroo	
15				do
16		tabemasu		
17			tanomoo	
18	tsukau			
19				sell
20				read

14

LESSON 3

	年	月	日
		曜日	番
名前			

(B) Unscramble the following words. The first 12 words are from Lessons 1 and 2; the others are from Volume One. The first letter of each word is given to help you. Words are in the same form as in the Sample Conversation.

1. bnziuu → z _____

2. tonooh → h _____

3. mkasiuak → k _____

4. kegni → g _____

5. aeighka → e _____

6. oktuosa → t _____

7. raweeit → i _____

8. aaaosnk → o _____

9. jaouboid → d _____

10. woase → o _____

11. irionobok → k _____

12. abeskoji → j _____

13. nnibuhs → s _____

14. ugiakad → d _____

15. nomistshu → s _____

16. sahiak → k _____

17. esmmuu → m _____

18. aakittaa → a _____

19. bsyiioou → s _____

20. mltusno → n _____

15

(C) Answer the following questions using *node* and the phrases in the parenthesis. The first phrase comes before *node*, and the second comes after *node*. Some of the words in the phrases need to be conjugated. Pay attention to the tenses used in the questions. Follow the example.

Example: *Sutiibu san, kongakki nihongo no seiseki wa taihen yokatta desu yo?*
スティーブさん、こんがっき　にほんごのせいせきは　たいへんよかったですよ。
(isshookenmei ganbaru ----- sore ga yokatta to omou)
Kongakki wa <u>isshookenmei ganbatta</u> node, <u>sore ga yokatta to omoimasu</u>.
こんがっきは　いっしょうけんめい　がんばったので、それが　よかったと　おもいます。

1. *Eiga wa doo deshita ka?*　えいがは　どうでしたか。
   (kowai shiin ga ooi ----- me o tsuburu [close]　こわいシーンが　おおい-----めを　つぶる)
   _____ *node, nankai mo* _____ .

2. *Kyoo no kibun wa ikaga desu ka?*　きょうの　きぶんは　いかがですか。
   (yuube shikkari neru ----- kibun ga ii　ゆうべ　しっかりねる-----きぶんが　いい)
   _____ *node, kyoo wa* _____ .

3. *Daikon* (Japanese radish) *no aji wa doo deshita ka?*　だいこんの　あじは　どうでしたか。
   (totemo karai ----- taberareru　とてもからい-----たべられる)
   _____ *node,* _____ .

4. *Kabuki wa doo deshita ka?*　かぶきは　どうでしたか。
   (seki ga suteeji kara tooi ----- yoku mieru　せきが　ステージからとおい-----よくみえる)
   _____ *node,* _____ .

5. *Mada okite iru n desu ka?*　まだ　おきているんですか。
   (koohii o nomisugiru ----- nemureru　コーヒーを　のみすぎる-----ねむれる)
   _____ *node, nakanaka* _____ .

16

LESSON 3

(D) Combine each pair of sentences using -nagara. The verb in the second sentence should be in the pre -nai form of the verb and followed by *nai de kudasai*, meaning "please do not ---." Then translate the sentence into English. Follow the example.

Example: *Shokuji o suru.   Terebi o miru.*   しょくじを　する。　　テレビを　みる。

Shokuji o shinagara terebi o minai de kudasai.

しょくじをしながら　テレビを　みないでください。

Don't watch TV while eating.

1. *Benkyoo suru.   Rajio o kiku.*   べんきょうする。　　ラジオを　きく。

_____   _____

_____

2. *Aruku.   Mono o taberu.*   あるく。　　ものを　たべる。

_____

_____

3. *Taberu.   Hanashi o suru.*   たべる。　　はなしをする。

_____

_____

4. *Hito no hanashi o kiku.   Shinbun o yomu.*   ひとのはなしを　きく。しんぶんを　よむ。

_____

_____

5. *Kuruma o unten suru   Keitaidenwa* (cellular telephone) *de hanasu.*

くるまを　うんてんする。　　けいたいでんわで　はなす。

_____

_____

17

LESSON 4

(A) Translate the following English words into Japanese and the Japanese words into English. Most of them are from Lesson 4; others are from Volume One.

	English	*Nihongo*
1	went	
2	schedule	
3	summer festival	
4	next	
5	wore	
6	finally	
7	Japanese summer kimono	
8	fast	
9	kitchen	
10	milk	
11		*ie*
12		*natsuyasumi*
13		*jugyoo*
14		*norimashita*
15		*kikitai*
16		*ohanashi*
17		*Nihon taiken*
18		*bon'odori*
19		*katamichi*
20		*ototoi*

LESSON 4

B) This exercise practices the use of yori in making comparisons. For each problem you are given two nouns and two adjectives. Using the two nouns, in any order, and one of the adjectives, write a comparative sentence according to the instructions. Try to be as creative as you can. Then translate your sentence into English. Follow the example.

Example: **words:** *taiheiyoo, indoyoo;   semai, hiroi*   **type:** Write a "yes/no" question.
   sentence: *Indoyoo wa taiheiyoo yori hiroi desu ka?*
         インドようは　たいへいようより　ひろいですか。
   translation: Is the Indian Ocean wider than the Pacific Ocean?

1. **words:** *Amazongawa, Mishishippiigawa;   nagai, mijikai*   **type:** Write a "yes/no" question.
   sentence: _____
   translation: _____

2. **words:** *pasuta, udon;   oishii, mazui*   **type:** Write a positive statement.
   sentence: _____
   translation: _____

3. **words:** *nezumi, neko;   ookii, chiisai*   **type:** Write a negative statement.
   sentence: _____
   translation: _____

4. **words:** *mashumaro, chokoreeto;   amai, nigai* (bitter)   **type:** Write a positive statement.
   sentence: _____
   translation: _____

5. **words:** *sakkaa no booru, yakyuu no booru;   katai, yawarakai* **type:** Write a negative statement.
   sentence: _____
   translation: _____

19

LESSON 4

年	月	日
	曜日	番
名前		

(C) Translate the following Japanese sentences into English.

1. *Motto Nihon no anime o mitai desu.*
   もっと　にほんのアニメを　みたいです。
   _____

2. *Motto hayaku hashirinasai.*
   もっとはやく　はしりなさい。
   _____

3. *Motto omoshiroi hanashi o shitte iru wa yo.*
   もっとおもしろいはなしを　しっているわよ。
   _____

4. *Minasan motto mae ni suwatte kudasai.*
   みなさん　もっとまえに　すわってください。
   _____

5. *Yuube osoku kaetta node motto nemuritai.*
   ゆうべおそく　かえったので　もっとねむりたい。
   _____

6. *Akachan ga nete iru kara motto shizuka ni shite kudasai.*
   あかちゃんが　ねているから　もっとしずかにしてください。
   _____

7. *Ojisan no hanashi wa omoshirokatta wa. Motto kikitai na.*
   おじさんのはなしは　おもしろかったわ。もっとききたいな。
   _____

8. *Anata wa motto motto benkyoo shinakereba ikemasen ne.*
   あなたは　もっともっと　べんきょうしなければいけませんね。
   _____

LESSON 4

年		月		日
	曜日			番
名前				

D) Match the phrases in List A with a phrase from List B to make meaningful sentences. Write the correct letter on the space provided. Each phrase in List B is used one time only.

LIST A   LIST B

_____ 1. *Kondo Nihon e ittara,*   a. *araimashoo ka?*
          こんど　にほんへいったら、   あらいましょうか。

_____ 2. *Shokuji ga owattara,*   b. *asobi ni ikimashoo ka?*
          しょくじが　おわったら、   あそびに　いきましょうか。

_____ 3. *Anata ga isogashii nara,*   c. *kabuki o mimashoo ka?*
          あなたが　いそがしいなら、   かぶきを　みましょうか。

_____ 4. *Jikan ni narimashita kara,*   d. *sukii ni ikimashoo ka?*
          じかんになりましたから、   スキーに　いきましょうか。

_____ 5. *Kono shastsu yogorete iru node,*   e. *resutoran de tabemashoo ka?*
          このシャツ　よごれているので、   レストランで　たべましょうか。

_____ 6. *Kono hon moo yonda kara,*   f. *koohii o iremashoo ka?*
          このほん　もうよんだから、   コーヒーを　いれましょうか。

_____ 7. *Ano geemu sonna ni hoshii nara,*   g. *toshokan ni kaeshimashoo ka?*
          あのゲーム　そんなにほしいなら、   としょかんに　かえしましょうか。

_____ 8. *Ie ni taberu mono ga nai node,*   h. *kaigi o hajimemashoo ka?*
          いえに　たべるものが　ないので、   かいぎを　はじめましょうか。

_____ 9. *Shiken ga owattara,*   i. *watashi no o urimashoo ka?*
          しけんが　おわったら、   わたしのを　うりましょうか。

_____ 10. *Yuki ga futte kita kara,*   j. *watashi ga kawari ni ikimashoo ka?*
          ゆきが　ふってきたから、   わたしが　かわりに　いきましょうか。

LESSON 5

年		月		日
		曜日		番
名前				

(A) Create your own original sentences using both of the given words. Verbs may be used in any tense, and the given words may be used in any order. Try to make sentences that are different from the Sample Conversation.

1. *tabi*　たび, *hajimete*　はじめて _____

   _____

2. *nemuru*　ねむる, *nanjikan*　なんじかん _____

   _____

3. *hikooki*　ひこうき, *koofun suru*　こうふんする _____

   _____

4. *tonikaku*　とにかく, *iku*　いく _____

   _____

5. *naka*　なか, *nemuru*　ねむる _____

   _____

6. *shitsumon*　しつもん, *shukudai*　しゅくだい _____

   _____

7. *sabishii*　さびしい, *oneesan*　おねえさん _____

   _____

8. *undookai*　うんどうかい, *nichiyoobi*　にちようび _____

   _____

年		月		日
		曜日		番
名前				

B) Using the expression --- *kamo shirenai/shiremasen*, write a response for each of the following sitiuations. Follow the example.

Example: Your newly born pet mouse is not moving this morning because of the cold weather.
    Shinda kamo shirenai.   しんだかも　しれない。

1. You are having problems with your computer, but you are unsuccessful in trying to fix it.

    _____

2. You are going to a party at a friend's house tonight, so you tell your parents that you might be late.

    _____

3. Your friend recommends a book to you but thinks that you may have already read it.

    _____

4. The sky is getting very dark and cloudy.

    _____

5. Today is Sunday, so you doubt that the store is open.

    _____

6. You think that your sister will get married next year.

    _____

7. You made chilli but think that it may be a little spicy.

    _____

	年		月		日
		曜日			番
名前					

(C) Using the expression --- *to ii desu yo*, give advice to the people in the following situations Follow the example.

Example: To a person who wants to make a long distance call but does not have enough change
      Korekuto kooru ni suru to ii desu yo. OR *Kooringu kaado o kau to ii desu yo*.
      コレクトコールにすると　いいですよ。　　コーリングカードをかうと　いいですよ。

1. To a friend who may be catching a cold.

    _____

2. To a classmate who is writing a report on sumo.

    _____

3. To your friend who wants to know the quickest way to send a package to Japan.

    _____

4. To a Japanese student who wants to know the zip code of a specific city.

    _____

5. To a friend who wants to go from New York City to Washington, DC.

    _____

6. To your host mother in Japan who wants to make a call when it is 8 p.m. in California.

    _____

7. To a Japanese friend who is interested in reading an American novel.

    _____

D) This exercise will help you remember how to refer to your own as well as someon else's family members. Complete the chart by filling in the blanks spaces with the correct name for each family member.

	English	My family	Someone else's family
1	father		
2			*okaasan*
3			*ojiisan*
4	grandmother		
5		*oji*	
6	aunt		
7		*ani*	
8			*oneesan*
9	younger brother		
10		*imooto*	
11	husband		
12			*okusan*

	年	月	日
	曜日		番
名前			

(A) The words listed in the box below are from Lessons 1, 2, 4, & 5. Group them into 7 different categories according to the given topic or hint. The number of blanks signifies the number of words that must be added to each group. Some words are listed to give you a hint for each category.

1. time: _____juunijikan_____ _____ _____ _____

_____

2. family: _____jibun_____ _____otooto_____ _____ _____

_____ _____

3. summer: _____natsuyasumi_____ _____ _____ _____

4. traveling: _____shashin_____ _____tabi_____ _____ _____

_____ _____ _____

5. adjectives: _____tanoshikatta_____ _____natsukashii_____ _____ _____

_____ _____

6. past tense verbs: _____norimashita_____ _____ _____ _____

7. dictionary form verbs: _____tsukau_____ _____kookan suru_____ _____ _____

_____

---

boku, bon'odori, daijoobu, ehagaki, genki, hayai, hikooki, ikimashita, iku, jisaboke, kimashita, nanjikan, neesan, niau, nittei, okaasan, omatsuri, omiyage, omoimashita, otoosan, owaru, sanshuukan, sensu, toki, ureshii, yukata

	年	月	日
	曜日		番
名前			

B) Create a two-line dialog in which A asks a question using --- *ni suru*. B will then answer the question, also using --- *ni suru*. For each problem you are given the type of question to use. Try to be creative. Follow the example.

Example: *dore ni suru*   どれにする

    A: *Kono omise no aisukuriimu mina oishisoo. Hiroko, dore ni suru?*
      このおみせの　アイスクリーム　みなおいしそう。ひろこ、どれにする。
    B: *Watashi wa banira ni suru wa.*
      わたしは　バニラにするわ。

1. *nani ni suru*   なににする

    A: _____ ?

    B: _____

2. *doko ni suru*   どこにする

    A: _____ ?

    B: _____

3. *dare ni suru*   だれにする

    A: _____ ?

    B: _____

4. *itsu ni suru*   いつにする

    A: _____ ?

    B: _____

5. *dochira ni suru*   どちらにする

    A: _____ ?

    B: _____

年	月	日
	曜日	番
名前		

(C) Answer the following questions using the expression --- *tari* --- *tari shimasu*. Follow the example.

Example: *Shuumatsu taitei nani o shimasu ka?* しゅうまつ　たいてい　なにをしますか。
　　　　 Shukudai o shitari, undoo o shitari shimasu. しゅくだいをしたり、うんどうをしたりします。

1. *Kodomo wa kaanibaru de nani o shite asobimasu ka?*
   こどもは　カーニバルで　なにをして　あそびますか。

   _____

2. *Natsu biichi de nani o shimasu ka?*
   なつ　ビーチで　なにをしますか。

   _____

3. *Kyanpu ni ittara nani o shimasu ka?*
   キャンプにいったら　なにをしますか。

   _____

4. *Amerika de wa kanshasai* (Thanksgiving) *no hi ni nani o shimasu ka?*
   アメリカでは　かんしゃさいのひに　なにをしますか。

   _____

5. *Nihon de wa oshoogatsu ni nani o shimasu ka?*
   にほんでは　おしょうがつに　なにをしますか。

   _____

6. *Kotoshi no natsuyasumi nani o shimasu ka?*
   ことしのなつやすみ　なにをしますか。

   _____

7. *Hawai ni ittara nani o shimasu ka?*
   ハワイにいったら　なにをしますか。

   _____

28

年	月	日
	曜日	番
名前		

D) The following expressions or phrases are related to one of the topics in the box below. Match each expression with the correct event and write the letter in the space provided.

A. GREETING CARDS	B. *YUKATA*
C. *NATSUMATSURI*	D. PUBLIC SAFETY

_____ 1. *taiko o tataku*   たいこを　たたく

_____ 2. *kootsuushingoo* (traffic light) *o mamoru*   こうつうしんごうを　まもる

_____ 3. *kazoku o tazuneru*   かぞくを　たずねる

_____ 4. *kitte o haru*   きってを　はる

_____ 5. *migigawa o aruku*   みぎがわを　あるく

_____ 6. *obi o shimeru*   おびを　しめる

_____ 7. *kuruma de hidarigawa o hashiru*   くるまで　ひだりがわを　はしる

_____ 8. *min'yoo* (folk music) *ni awasete odoru*   みんように　あわせて　おどる

_____ 9. *watagashi o taberu*   わたがしを　たべる

_____ 10. *fuutoo* (envelope) *ni ireru*   ふうとうに　いれる

_____ 11. *uchiwa* (fan) *o tsukau*   うちわを　つかう

_____ 12. *hagaki o dasu*   はがきを　だす

_____ 13. *ohakamairi o suru*   おはかまいりをする

_____ 14. *chuusha ihan* (parking violation) *o shinai*   ちゅうしゃいはんを　しない

_____ 15. *tegami o kaku*   てがみを　かく

_____ 16. *geta o haku*   げたを　はく

_____ 17. *hanabi o miru*   はなびを　みる

_____ 18. *seigen* (limit) *supiido o mamoru*   せいげんスピードを　まもる

29

| | | 年 | | 月 | | 日 |

| | 曜日 | | 番 |

| 名前 | |

(A) Find and circle 12 words from Lesson 7 that are hidden in the chart below. They are written horizontally, vertically, diagonally, and backwards. There is no word list.

A	T	O	F	O	K	U	G	E	O
K	I	A	T	A	Y	H	O	T	K
T	E	O	D	A	M	U	S	U	A
I	S	K	U	Y	K	T	O	S	B
G	O	O	I	A	H	A	K	I	J
A	T	I	K	R	S	N	A	A	S
R	I	I	Y	E	O	N	T	K	E
O	H	R	U	M	N	O	T	U	K
C	M	I	T	A	I	P	A	S	R
E	Y	U	P	K	D	M	E	T	I

年	月	日
	曜日	番
名前		

3) In the spaces provided, conjugate the verbs in the chart into the *-te* form. Using the sentence
    pattern *Kore o -te ii?*, translate each sentence into English. Follow the example.

Example: *yomu* → *yonde*   (*Kore o yonde ii?*)   May I read this?

#	Dictionary Form	*-te* Form	English Translation
1	akeru		
2	arau		
3	hajimeru		
4	iu		
5	kaesu		
6	kaku		
7	kau		
8	kesu		
9	kiku		
10	(kami o) kiru		
11	(kimono o) kiru		
12	miru		
13	nomu		
14	noru		
15	okuru		
16	taberu		
17	toru		
18	tsukau		

(C) In this exercise, a friend expresses a situation or a desire to do something. Write a good suggestion for each case using the expressing --- *tara*. Follow the example.

Example: A: *Kaze o hiita mitai.*　　かぜをひいた　みたい。

B: <u>*Konya wa hayaku netara.*</u>　　<u>こんやは　はやくねたら。</u>

1. A: *Kantan na chooshoku o toritai n desu kedo.* かんたんな　ちょうしょくを　とりたいんですけど。

B: _____

2. A: *Nodo ga kawaita na.*　　のどが　かわいたな。

B: _____

3. A: *Nani ka supootsu o hajimetai n desu ga.*　　なにか　スポーツを　はじめたいんですが。

B: _____

4. A: *Kondo wa eigo o hanasu kuni e ryokoo shitai wa.*
こんどは　えいごをはなす　くにへ　りょこうしたいわ。

B: _____

5. A: *Doko ka yasui tiishatsu o utte iru omise wa nai?*
どこか　やすいティーシャツを　うっている　おみせはない。

B: _____

6. A: *Kondo no shuumatsu omoshiroi eiga ga mitai na.*
こんどのしゅうまつ　おもしろいえいがが　みたいな。

B: _____

7. A: *Nihon no omiyage nani ni shiyoo?*　　にほんのおみやげ　なににしよう。

B: _____

LESSON 8

<table>
<tr><td></td><td>年</td><td>月</td><td>日</td></tr>
<tr><td></td><td colspan="2">曜日</td><td>番</td></tr>
<tr><td>名前</td><td colspan="3"></td></tr>
</table>

A) Complete the following sentences by filling in the blanks with words or phrases from Lesson 8.

1. *Gakkoo wa ie kara* _____ *desu. Aruite 5fun desu.*

   がっこうは　いえから_____です。あるいて　5ふんです。

2. *Nara no* _____ *o mi ni ikitai.*

   ならの_____を　みにいきたい。

3. *Watashi no* _____ *naka no yoi tomodachi no namae wa Maiku desu.*

   わたしの_____なかのよい　ともだちのなまえは　マイクです。

4. *Eberesutozan wa* _____ *de ichiban takai yama desu.*

   エベレストざんは_____で　いちばんたかいやまです。

5. *Kyooto de wa* _____ *ie to otera ga ooi soo desu.*

   きょうとでは_____いえと　おてらが　おおいそうです。

6. *Nyuu Yooku ni aru* _____ *o mi ni* _____?

   ニューヨークにある_____をみに_____。

7. *Koko kara Nihon made wa hikooki de juujikan* _____ *desu.*

   ここから　にほんまでは　ひこうきで　じゅうじかん_____です。

8. *Ejiputo no piramiddo wa itsu goro* _____ *to omoimasu ka?*

   エジプトの　ピラミッドは　いつごろ_____とおもいますか。

9. *Yuubinkyoku e iku kara* _____ *ni kusuriya ni itte kimashoo ka?*

   ゆうびんきょくへ　いくから_____に　くすりやに　いってきましょうか。

0. *Nihon e ittara* _____ *osushi o tabetai.*

   にほんへいったら_____おすしをたべたい。

33

(B) Complete the sentences by filling in the blanks with the given words or phrases for each question. As in the example, make sure you conjugate the verbs with-*masen*.

Example: *tenisu* ----- *suru*　テニス-----する

　　　　Kondo no doyoobi <u>tenisu o shimasen</u> ka?　こんどのどようび　テニスをしませんか。

1. *Kororado* ----- *sukii ni iku*　コロラド-----スキーにいく

   3gatsu no haruyasumi ni _____ka?

   ３がつの　はるやすみに _____ か。

2. *atatakai mono* ----- *taberu*　あたたかいもの-----たべる

   Kyoo wa samui kara _____ka?

   きょうは　さむいから _____ か。

3. *Nihon no bideo* ----- *miru*　にほんのビデオ-----みる

   Kondo no nichiyoobi watashi no ie de _____ka?

   こんどのにちようび　わたしのいえで _____ か。

4. *boku no yukata* ----- *kiru*　ぼくのゆかた-----きる

   Asu no bon'odori ni wa _____ka?

   あすの　ぼんおどりには _____ か。

5. *watashi no kurabu* ----- *tsukau*　わたしのクラブ-----つかう

   Gorufu ga yaritai nara _____ka?

   ゴルフが　やりたいなら _____ か。

6. *jettokoosutaa* ----- *noru*　ジェットコースター-----のる

   Kowasoo dakedo ichido _____ka?

   こわそうだけど　いちど _____ か。

7. *watashi no ie* ----- *kuru*　わたしのいえ-----くる

   Raigetsu no omatsuri no hi _____ka?

   らいげつの　おまつりのひ _____ か。

34

LESSON 8

C) Change sentences 1-5 from the active to the passive form and sentences 6-10 from passive to active.

1. *Ooku no hito ga kono hon o yomimashita.*   おおくのひとが　このほんを　よみました。

   _____

2. *Shichoo san* (mayor) *wa 3nin no gakusei o hyooshoo shimashita.*
   しちょうさんは　3にんのがくせいを　ひょうしょうしました。

   _____

3. *Keijiban* (message board) *ni ironna hito ga dengon memo o hatte imasu.*
   けいじばんに　いろんなひとが　でんごんメモを　はっています。

   _____

4. *Konshuu wa 1jikan hayaku yuuenchi no mon o akete imasu.*
   こんしゅうは　1じかんはやく　ゆうえんちのもんを　あけています。

   _____

5. *Gogo 3ji kara LA Myuujikku wa shinkyoku o happyoo shimasu.*
   ごご3じから　LAミュージックは　しんきょくを　はっぴょうします。

   _____

6. *30nen mae no taimu kapuseru ga akerareta.*   30ねんまえの　タイムカプセルが　あけられた。

   _____

7. *Kono tatemono wa 1997nen ni taterareta.*   このたてものは　1997ねんに　たてられた。

   _____

8. *Shokuji no toki itsumo ocha ga dasaremasu.*   しょくじのとき　いつも　おちゃが　だされます。

   _____

9. *Kyoo no gesuto supiikaa wa takusan shitsumon saremashita.*
   きょうの　ゲストスピーカーは　たくさん　しつもんされました。

   _____

10. *Piitaa wa Nanshii ni damasaremashita.*
    ピーターは　ナンシーに　だまされました。

    _____

	年	月	日
		曜日	番
名前			

(D) Change each of the phrases in the box below into a question using the pattern -nai no? The match the questions with the following answers. Write the questions in the space provided Follow the example.

Example: A: *Kuruma de ikanai no?*　　くるまで　いかないの。

　　　　 B: *Ima no jikan mada rasshu awaa dakara densha ga hayai to omou yo.*
　　　　　 いまのじかん　まだラッシュアワーだから　でんしゃが　はやいとおもうよ。

1.　A: _____ ?

　　B: *Sensei ni kiitara kyoo de nakute mo ii soo yo.*
　　　 せんせいに　きいたら　きょうでなくても　いいそうよ。

2.　A: _____ ?

　　B: *Kakoo to omotta kedo, binsen* (letter paper) *ga nai n da.*
　　　 かこうとおもったけど、びんせんがないんだ。

3.　A: _____ ?

　　B: *Mada ie ni modotte inai to omou kara moo sukoshi ato ni suru yo.*
　　　 まだ　いえにもどっていない　とおもうから　もうすこしあとにするよ。

4.　A: _____ ?

　　B: *Onaka ga amari suite inai node kono shigoto ga owatte kara ni suru yo.*
　　　 おなかが　あまりすいていないので　このしごとが　おわってからにするよ。

5.　A: _____ ?

　　B: *Minna onaji tabemono ja tsumarai kara.*
　　　 みんな　おなじたべものじゃ　つまらないから。

6.　A: _____ ?

　　B: *Moo sukoshi asonde kaeritai kara saki ni kaette.*
　　　 もうすこし　あそんでかえりたいから　さきにかえって。

Denwa o kakeru. でんわをかける。	*Shukudai wa kyoo dasu.* しゅくだいは　きょう　だす。
Mariko wa piza ni suru. まりこは　ピザにする。	
Shokuji ni suru. しょくじにする。	*Kuruma de iku.* くるまでいく。
Tegami o kaku. てがみをかく。	*Naomi wa mada kaeru.* なおみは　まだかえる。

LESSON 9

年	月	日
	曜日	番
名前		

A) Fill in the blank spaces of the following verb conjugation chart. The verbs are from Lessons 4, 5, 7, and 8 as well as from Volume One.

#	Dictionary Form	-tara Form	Pre -masu + tai	English: -tai
1	dekakeru			
2			ikitai	
3			kaeritai	
4				want to lend
5		kattara		
6			kikitai	
7	kimeru			
8				want to wear
9		kitara		
10	magaru			
11		mitara		
12				want to have, hold
13	naku			
14			nemuritai	
15				want to ride, go by
16				want to get up
17	suru			
18			tazunetai	
19	yasumu			
20			yobitai	

年		月		日
	曜日			番
名前				

(B) Complete the following crossword puzzle. Words and clues are taken mostly from Lessons 7 and 8. All answers are in Japanese. For English clues in quotations, the answer is the Japanese translation.

ACROSS

7. "number one"
8. "the world"
9. *Chotto atsui node, _____ o akete kudasai.*
11. *Tookyoo e _____ no?*
13. *Donna eiga o _____ desu ka?*
15. *Daibutsu wa _____ ni dekimashita.*
16. "I forgot!"

DOWN

1. *Emirii wa gakkoo no _____ ni sunde imasu*
2. *_____! Okane o wasurechatta.*
3. *Ano _____ wa watashi no ojisan da yo.*
4. *_____ wa chiisai sakana daro.*
5. *Omatsuri de wa _____ ga takusan deru yo*
6. "definitely"
10. opposite of "early"
12. *Bon'odori o shita toki, yukata o _____.*
14. *Gakkoo wa 1935 ni dekita _____ biru da yo*

年		月		日
		曜日		番
名前				

C) Translate the following English sentences into Japanese.

1. He would like to speak Japanese fluently (*joozu ni*).

   _____

2. He would like to work at the American consulate (*ryoojikan*) in Japan.

   _____

3. I want to be a Japanese interpreter (*tsuuyaku*).

   _____

4. I want to read a Japanese book without a dictionary.

   _____

5. I want to learn Japanese pottery (*yakimono*).

   _____

6. She wants to make sushi by herself.

   _____

7. She wants to wear a *kimono* someday.

   _____

8. They would like to visit Kyoto, Nara, and Tokyo this year.

   _____

9. They would like to eat *zooni* for this coming *oshoogatsu*.

   _____

10. They would like to watch sumo in Japan.

   _____

LESSON 9

(D) Fill in the blanks of the following sentences with the most appropriate word or expression from those listed in the box below in order to match with the English translation.

1. *Kare wa hito no warukuchi (*　　　　　　　) *itte iru.*

   かれは　ひとのわるくち（　　　　　　　）いっている。

   He always speaks ill of others.

2. *(*　　　　　　) *kyoo mi ni ikitai na.*

   （　　　　　　）きょう　みにいきたいな。

   But I would like to go see it today.

3. A: *(*　　　　　　*), kono kiihoorudaa wa watashi no da wa.*

   （　　　　　　）このキーホルダーは　わたしのだわ。

   Why, this keyholder is mine!

   B: *Otearai ni okiwasurete imashita yo.*

   おてあらいに　おきわすれていましたよ。

   You left it in the restroom.

   A: *(*　　　　　　*), soo deshita ka?*

   （　　　　　　）、そうでしたか。

   Oh, really?

4. *(*　　　　　　*). Minna sansei shiteru kara soo shimashoo.*

   （　　　　　　）。みんな　さんせいしてるから　そうしましょう。

   That's right. Everyone agrees, so let's do that.

5. *(*　　　　　　*) soo datta no ne.*

   （　　　　　　）そうだったのね。

   It's as I had supposed, isn't it?

ara あら	*bakari* ばかり	*demo* でも	*maa* まあ	*soo ne* そうね
yappari やっぱり				

	年	月	日
	曜日		番
名前			

A) Create your own original sentences using both of the given words. Verbs may be used in any tense, and the given words may be used in any order. Try to make sentences that are different from the Sample Conversation.

1. *gogo* ごご, *gozen* ごぜん _____

_____

2. *daitokai* だいとかい, *hiru* ひる _____

_____

3. *tokoro* ところ, *yoru* よる _____

_____

4. *ame* あめ, *tenkiyohoo* てんきよほう _____

_____

5. *kuji* くじ, *hare* はれ _____

_____

6. *shichiji* しちじ, *hanasu* はなす _____

_____

7. *kuruma* くるま, *kookoosei* こうこうせい _____

_____

8. *megane* めがね, *komaru* こまる

_____

	年	月	日
		曜日	番
名前			

(B) Fill in the blanks of the following sentences with a verb from the box below. Conjugate the verbs according to the example.

Example: *Yukata o ___kite iru___ onna no hito wa minna utsukushiku miemasu.*

ゆかたを＿きている＿おんなのひとは　みんなうつくしくみえます。

1. *Asoko de denwa o _____ hito ni sugu kuru yoo ni tsutaete kudasai.*

あそこででんわを＿＿＿＿＿＿＿＿＿＿ひとに　すぐくるように　つたえてください。

2. *Kotchi ni te o _____ otoko no hito wa uchi no otoosan ja nai?*

こっちに　てを＿＿＿＿＿＿＿＿＿＿おとこのひとは　うちのおとうさんじゃない。

3. *Achira no teeburu de hon o _____ gakusei wa Nihon kara*

_____ *ryuugakusei desu.*

あちらのテーブルで　ほんを＿＿＿＿＿＿＿＿＿がくせいは　にほんから＿＿＿＿＿＿＿＿＿

りゅうがくせいです。

4. *Kuruma o _____ no wa uchi no obaachan desu.*

くるまを＿＿＿＿＿＿＿＿＿＿のは　うちのおばあちゃんです。

5. *Sushi o _____ hito ga watashi no kare desu.*

すしを＿＿＿＿＿＿＿＿＿＿ひとが　わたしのかれです。

6. *Shashin o _____ josei wa Amerika no jaanarisuto desu ka?*

しゃしんを＿＿＿＿＿＿＿＿＿＿じょせいは　アメリカのジャーナリストですか。

7. *Kyoo wa tenki ga ii node kooen o _____ hito ga ooi desu ne.*

きょうは　てんきがいいので　こうえんを＿＿＿＿＿＿＿＿＿ひとがおおいですね。

aruku あるく	*furu* ふる	*hanasu* はなす	*kakeru* かける
kaku かく	*kiru* きく	*kuru* くる	*oyogu* およぐ
taberu たべる	*toru* とる	*yomu* よむ	*unten suru* うんてんする

LESSON 10

年	月	日
	曜日	番
名前		

C1) Fill in the blank of each sentence with as many different adjectives as you can. The sentences should be meaningful. Follow the example.

Example: *Tookyoo wa* __ii; tanoshii; hito ga ooi__ *tokoro desu.*

1. *Hokkaidoo wa* _____ *tokoro desu.*

2. *Okinawa wa* _____ *tokoro desu.*

3. *Nyuu Yooku wa* _____ *tokoro desu.*

4. *Nihon no inaka wa* _____ *tokoro desu.*

5. *Rasu Begasu wa* _____ *tokoro desu.*

C2) In the following sentences, fill in the first blank with an adjective or an adjectival noun plus *na* and the second blank with a noun. The sentences should be meaningful. Follow the example.

Example: *Tookyoo wa* __tanoshii__ __basho__ *desu.*

1. *Mango wa* _____ _____ *desu.*

2. *"Za Ekkusu Fairuzu" wa* _____ _____ *desu.*

3. *Amerika wa* _____ _____ *desu.*

4. *Futtobooru wa* _____ _____ *desu.*

5. *Konpyuutaa wa* _____ _____ *desu.*

6. *Koinu* (puppy) *wa* _____ _____ *desu.*

7. *Sanpurasu* (Sampras) *wa* _____ _____ *desu.*

43

LESSON 11

(A) Complete the following sentences with words or phrases from Lesson 11.

1. *Osushi wa watashi no* _____ *na tabemono desu.*

   おすしは　わたしの_____な　たべものです。

2. *Kazoku to issho ni* _____ *o torimashita.*

   かぞくといっしょに_____を　とりました。

3. _____ *wa daigakusei desu ka?*

   _____は　だいがくせいですか。

4. *Nattoo ga suki desu ga,* _____ *wa chotto.....*

   なっとうが　すきですが、_____は　ちょっと。。。

5. *Kinoo dezaato o takusan tabeta node, chotto* _____ *kamo shirenai.*

   きのう　デザートを　たくさんたべたので、ちょっと_____かもしれない。

6. *Kore wa nan to iu* _____ *desu ka?*

   これは　なんという_____ですか。

7. *Nihon ryokoo no* _____ *no hi wa nani o shitai desu ka?*

   にほんりょこうの_____のひは　なにをしたいですか。

8. *Otoosan wa tokidoki osoku ie ni* _____.

   おとうさんは　ときどき　おそくいえに_____。

9. *Nihon no omise de wa iriguchi no doa wa* _____ *de akimasu.*

   にほんのおみせでは　いりぐちのドアは_____で　あきます。

10. _____ *ga aru hito wa resutoran de nani o tabetara ii ka komarimasu.*

    _____があるひとは　レストランで　なにをたべたらいいか　こまります。

44

(B) Using *node* and *kamo shirenai*, combine sentences A and B to create a new sentence. Pay attention to the sentence pattern and tenses used in the example.

Example: A: *Takusan taberu.*   B: *Futoru.*
            たくさん　たべる 　　　　　　ふとる。
            Takusan tabeta node, futotta kamo shirenai.
            たくさん　たべたので、ふとったかもしれない。

1.   A: *Mainichi renshuu suru.*   B: *Joozu ni naru.*
      まいにち　れんしゅうする。 　　　　　じょうずになる。

_____

2.   A: *Maiasa jogingu suru.*   B: *Yaseru.*
      まいあさ　ジョギングする 　　　　　　やせる。

_____

3.   A: *Isoide kaku.*   B: *Machigai ga ooi.*
      いそいで　かく。 　　　　　　　　　　まちがいが　おおい。

_____

4.   A: *30pun mo osoku ie o deru.*   B: *Chikoku suru.*
      ３０ぷんもおそく　いえを　でる。 　　ちこくする。

_____

5.   A: *Doru ga tsuyoku naru.*   B: *Kaigairyokoo wa yasuku naru.*
      ドルが　つよくなる。 　　　　　　　　かいがいりょこうは　やすくなる。

_____

6.   A: *Ooyuki ga furu.*   B: *Hikooki ga okureru.*
      おおゆきが　ふる。 　　　　　　　　　ひこうきが　おくれる。

_____

7.   A: *Onaka ga itai.*   B: *Gakkoo o yasumu*
      おなかが　いたい。 　　　　　　　　　がっこうを　やすむ。

_____

	年	月	日
	曜日		番
名前			

(C) Match the following questions or statements with one of the reasons listed in the box below. Write the correct reason on the line provided.

1. *Kinenshashin o torimasen ka?* _____
   きねんしゃしんを　とりませんか。

2. *Issho ni benkyoo shimasen ka?* _____
   いっしょに　べんきょうしませんか。

3. *Kono uta minna kikitai to omoimasu yo.* _____
   このうた　みんな　ききたいとおもいますよ。

4. *Genki o dashite ganbarimashoo.* _____
   げんきを　だして　がんばりましょう。

5. *Atarashii no to kaete morattara.* _____
   あたらしいのと　かえてもらったら。

6. *Kuruma made hakonde* (carry) *kuremasen ka?* _____
   くるま　まで　はこんでくれませんか。

7. *Kyoo no chuushoku wa kooen de tabemasen ka?* _____
   きょうのちゅうしょくは　こうえんで　たべませんか。

8. *Senshuu kashita bideo hayaku kaeshite yo.* _____
   せんしゅう　かしたビデオ　はやくかえしてよ。

REASONS

Ato moo sukoshi dakara.　　あと　もうすこしだから。

Ima besuto-ten ni haitte iru uta dakara.　　いま　ベストテンにはいっている　うただから。

Katta bakari nan dakara.　　かったばかり　なんだから。

Kyoo ga saigo dakara.　　きょうが　さいごだから。

Raishuu no kimatsushiken wa muzukashisoo dakara.
らいしゅうの　きまつしけんは　むずかしそうだから。

Taihen omosoo dakara.　　たいへん　おもそうだから。

Tenki mo ii shi atatakasoo dakara.　　てんきもいいし　あたたかそうだから。

Watashi wa mada mite inai n dakara.　　わたしは　まだ　みていないんだから。

LESSON 12

年	月	日
	曜日	番
名前		

(A) In the space provided, write the antonym of each of the following words.

1. *onna*   おんな   ⟷   _____

2. *otooto*   おとうと   ⟷   _____

3. *kirai*   きらい   ⟷   _____

4. *oneesan*   おねえさん   ⟷   _____

5. *soto*   そと   ⟷   _____

6. *owaru*   おわる   ⟷   _____

7. *ookii*   おおきい   ⟷   _____

8. *atarashii* あたらしい   ⟷   _____

9. *gogo*   ごご   ⟷   _____

10. *natsu*   なつ   ⟷   _____

11. *yoru*   よる   ⟷   _____

12. *chikai*   ちかい   ⟷   _____

13. *hayai*   はやい   ⟷   _____

14. *okiru*   おきる   ⟷   _____

15. *isoi de*   いそいで   ⟷   _____

16. *wasureru*   わすれる   ⟷   _____

17. *haha*   はは   ⟷   _____

18. *yawarakai* やわらかい   ⟷   _____

19. *kanashii*   かなしい   ⟷   _____

(B) First choose a verb from the box below that best completes each sentence, conjugate it according to the example, and write it in the parenthesis. Then translate each sentence in the space provided. Each verb is used only once.

Example: *Orinpikku wa moo (owarimashita) ka?* オリンピックはもう（おわりました）か。

Have the Oylmpics already ended?; Are the Olympics already over?

1. *Chuushoku moo (   ) ka?*
   ちゅうしょく　もう(   )か。

   _____

2. *Hiroshi kun, shukudai wa moo (   ) ka?*
   ひろしくん、しゅくだいはもう(   )か。

   _____

3. *Kusuri wa moo (   ) ka?*
   くすりはもう(   )か。

   _____

4. *Kyoo wa moo kaimono ni (   ).*
   きょうはもう　かいものに(   )。

   _____

5. *Omise wa moo (   ).*
   おみせは　もう(   )。

   _____

6. *Kondo no eiga moo (   ) ka?*
   こんどのえいが　もう(   )か。

   _____

48

	年	月	日
		曜日	番
名前			

7. *Watashi wa moo fuyufuku o (*   *) yo.*
    わたしはもう　ふゆふくを（　　　　　　　）よ。

_____

8. *Piitaa san wa moo gakkoo ni (*   *) ka?*
    ピーターさんはもう　がっこうに（　　　　　）か。

_____

9. *Satomi san wa moo ie ni (*   *) ka?*
    さとみさんはもう　いえに（　　　　　）か。

_____

10. *Anata wa moo reshiito ni (*   *) ka?*
    あなたはもう　レシートに（　　　　　）か。

_____

---

dasu だす, *dekakeru* でかける, *iku* いく, *kaeru* かえる, *miru* みる, *nomu* のむ, *owaru* おわる, *sain* サイン, *suru* する, *shimaru* しまる, *suru* する, *taberu* たべる

LESSON 12

(C) In Japanese, there is a significant difference between formal and informal speech. For each of the following sentences, write an F in the blank if the sentence is formal, or write an I if it is informal.

_____ 1. *Otoosan no byooki no guai wa doo datta?*
おとうさんの　びょうきのぐあいは　どうだった。

_____ 2. *Asu wa yuki ni naru deshoo.*
あすは　ゆきに　なるでしょう。

_____ 3. *Kinoo wa taihen na ooame deshita ne.*
きのうは　たいへんな　おおあめでしたね。

_____ 4. *Sono sangurasu wa 2man en wa suru daroo.*
そのサングラスは　２まんえんは　するだろう。

_____ 5. *Kono fuku wa tashika itariasei desu.*
このふくは　たしか　イタリアせいです。

_____ 6. *Ashita wa kitto hareru yo.*
あしたは　きっと　はれるよ。

_____ 7. *Kaigi ni shusseki shita hito wa tashika 25nin desu.*
かいぎにしゅっせきしたひとは　たしか　２５にんです。

_____ 8. *Nihon de mo intaanetto o tsukau hito ga fuetasoo da.*
にほんでも　インターネットを　つかうひとが　ふえたそうだ。

_____ 9. *Koobe de jishin ga atta no wa 3nen mae no kinoo deshita.*
こうべで　じしんがあったのは　３ねんまえのきのうでした。

_____ 10. *Watashi no ryooshin wa futari to mo kookoosei no toki supootsu senshu datta.*
わたしのりょうしんは　ふたりとも　こうこうせいのとき　スポーツせんしゅだった。

_____ 11. *Sore tte kyonen no hanashi da yo ne.*
それって　きょねんのはなしだよね。

_____ 12. *Sono toori desu.*
そのとおりです。

_____ 13. *Tanaka san, buchoo ga oyobi desu. Sugu kite hoshii soo desu.*
たなかさん、ぶちょうが　およびです。すぐきてほしいそうです。

_____ 14. *Pikunikku no ken, ame ga futtara doo suru?*
ピクニックのけん、あめがふったら　どうする。

LESSON 12

年	月	日
	曜日	番
名前		

(D) In each of the following lists there is one item that does not belong to the specified category. Circle the incorrect word and then try to think of another item to replace it. Write the new word in the parenthesis.

1. *YATAI*: (   )

   okonomiyaki, kingyosukui, unagi, watagashi, ringoame
   おこのみやき、きんぎょすくい、うなぎ、わたがし、りんごあめ

2. DISPOSABLE GOODS: (   )

   hashi, nabe, supuun, fooku, sara   はし、なべ、スプーン、フォーク、さら

3. CITIES ON HONSHU: (   )

   Nara, Kyooto, Tookyoo, Sapporo, Oosaka   なら、きょうと、とうきょう、さっぽろ、おおさか

4. TELEPHONE CONVERSATION EXPRESSIONS: (   )

   Dochira sama desu ka, Shooshoo omachi kudasai, Bangoo ga chigaimasu, Doozo oagari kudasai
   どちらさまですか、しょうしょう　おまちください、ばんごうがちがいます、どうぞ　おあがりください

5. SIGHTSEEING: (   )

   Mitsukoshi, Miyajima, Tookyoo Dizuniirando, Kinkakuji, Hakone
   みつこし、みやじま、とうきょうディズニーランド、きんかくじ、はこね

6. JAPANESE FOOD: (   )

   tenpura, gyooza, soba, udon, sukiyaki   てんぷら、ギョーザ、そば、うどん、すきやき

7. TOKYO: (   )

   Shinjuku, Asakusa, Meijimura, Meijijinguu, Uenokooen
   しんじゅく、あさくさ、めいじむら、めいじじんぐう、うえのこうえん

LESSON 13

(A) Translate the following English words into Japanese and the Japanese words into English. Most of them are from Lesson 13; others are from Volume One.

	English	*Nihongo*
1		*menzeiten*
2		*ryokoo*
3		*sagaseba*
4		*kondo*
5		*eigo*
6		*ototoshi*
7		*umareru*
8		*kusuriya*
9		*kekkonshiki*
10		*subarashii*
11	anything	
12	charm	
13	in an instant	
14	half	
15	Japanese doll	
16	classroom	
17	Sea of Japan	
18	building	
19	to take pictures	
20	subway	

	年	月	日
		曜日	番
名前			

B) In each of the following problems, a friend of yours is in a situation where he/she needs some advice. Give a suggestion by using the expression *-eba ii desu yo*, following the example.

Example: *Furui eiga o mitai toki, doo sureba ii deshoo ka?*
　　　　ふるいえいがを　みたいとき、どうすればいいでしょうか。
　　　　Bideo o mireba ii desu yo.　　ビデオをみればいいですよ。

1. *Nihongo no tango no imi ga wakaranai toki, doo sureba ii deshoo ka?*
　にほんごの　たんごのいみが　わからないとき、どうすればいいでしょうか？

　_____

2. *Onaka ga itai toki, doo sureba ii deshoo ka?*
　おなかが　いたいとき、どうすればいいでしょうか。

　_____

3. *Mooru ni ikitai toki wa, doo sureba ii deshoo ka?*
　モールに　いきたいときは、どうすればいいでしょうか

　_____

4. *Tsukareta toki, doo sureba ii deshoo ka?*
　つかれたとき、どうすればいいでしょうか。

　_____

5. *Michi ni mayotta* (get lost) *toki, doo sureba ii deshoo ka?*
　みちにまよったとき、どうすればいいでしょうか。

　_____

6. *Piano o joozu ni hikitai toki, doo sureba ii deshoo ka?*
　ピアノを　じょうずに　ひきたいとき、どうすればいいでしょうか。

　_____

年	月	日
	曜日	番
名前		

(C) First complete the sentences in the box below by filling in the blanks with an appropriate verb in the -*te* form. Then for each of the following situations, choose the most suitable response from the completed sentences in the box. Write the letter on the line next to the correct situation.

Example: __c__ A boy helps his grandmother by carrying a heavy box for her.....

SITUATIONS

_____ 1. You are leaving your friend's house after having been invited to stay for dinner and say ...

_____ 2. You and your friends are heading towards the train platform, but you want to stop to buy a soda. Your friends waited for you. You say ...

_____ 3. You helped your mother wash the dishes. She says ...

_____ 4. Your grandfather has to go to the doctor, so you drove him. He says ...

_____ 5. You were too busy to go to the market, so your brother went for you. Later you say ...

_____ 6. You borrowed your friend's dictionary all day. When you return it you say ...

RESPONSES

a. *Katte* _____ *kurete arigatoo.*　　かって_____くれて　ありがとう。

b. *Kono jisho* _____ *kurete arigatoo.*　このじしょ_____くれて　ありがとう。

c. *Omoi nimotsu* _____o motte_____ *kurete hontoo ni arigatoo.*

　おもいにもつ<u>をもって</u>くれて　ほんとうにありがとう。

d. *Kuruma de* _____ *kurete arigatoo.*　くるまで_____くれて　ありがとう。

e. *Kyoo wa* _____ *kurete arigatoo. Totemo tanoshikatta wa.*

　きょうは_____くれて　ありがとう。とても　たのしかったわ。

f. *Osara* _____ *kurete tasukatta wa.*　おさら_____くれて　たすかったわ。

g. *Matte* _____ *kurete arigatoo.*　　まって_____くれて　ありがとう。

54

	年	月	日
		曜日	番
名前			

A) Unscramble the following words. The first 8 are from Lesson 14; the others are from lessons 4 through 13. The first letter of each word is given to help you. Words are in the same form as in the Sample Conversation.

1. agiijkknou → g _____

2. sihhoi → h _____

3. nkmiooa → k _____

4. sahiaatir → a _____

5. snnkiiiheed → d _____

6. eonosi → s _____

7. aysora → s _____

8. riketu → k _____

9. roionodb → b _____

10. aaiiokdt → d _____

11. aaijknnn → n _____

12. ikutanok → t _____

13. tatotuf → f _____

14. ayakarem → k _____

15. iainson → o _____

16. mmirooa → o _____

17. imtjehea → h _____

18. muenur → n _____

19. iktiaik → k _____

20. okihiok → h _____

	年	月	日
	曜日		番
名前			

(B) Look at the numbered family chart below. In each case "you" will be assigned a different number. Determine how the numbers listed for each problem are related to you. In the box below is an alphabetical list of the names of family members that you may need to do this exercise. Note: In the family chart, for siblings or spouses, the person farthest to the left is the oldest. In other words, the oldest person has the lowest number.

Example: You are 17........   13: _otoosan_

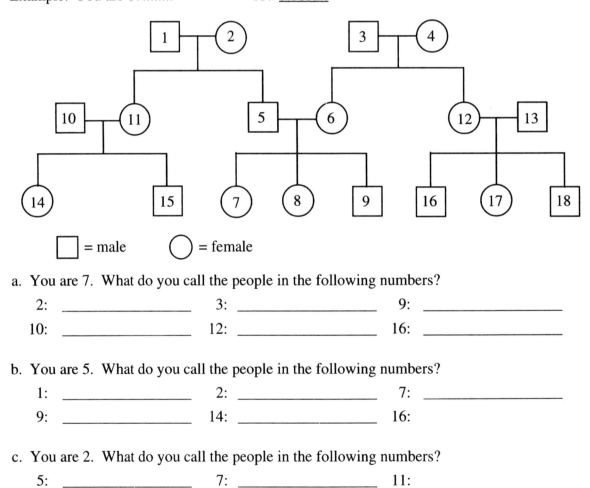

☐ = male   ◯ = female

a. You are 7. What do you call the people in the following numbers?

   2: _____   3: _____   9: _____

  10: _____   12: _____   16: _____

b. You are 5. What do you call the people in the following numbers?

   1: _____   2: _____   7: _____

   9: _____   14: _____   16: _____

c. You are 2. What do you call the people in the following numbers?

   5: _____   7: _____   11:

d. You are 15. What do you call the people in the following numbers?

   2: _____   8: _____   14: _____

---

imooto, itoko, mago (grandchild), _mei_ (neice), _musuko, musume, obaasan, obasan, oi_ (nephew), _ojiisan, ojisan, okaasan, oneesan, oniisan, otoosan, otooto_

(C) Read the following sentences and determine whether the speaker is male or female. Write M in the blank if the sentence is spoken by a male or F if it is spoken by a female. If the sentence could be said by both men and women, then write B.

_____ 1. *Kono hon totemo omoshirokatta wa.*
このほん　とても　おもしろかったわ。

_____ 2. *Kochira no CD wa 20paasento nebiki shite orimasu.*
こちらのCDは　２０パーセント　ねびきしております。

_____ 3. *Sochira no sokkusu wa 3zoku de 200en de gozaimsu.*
そちらのソックスは　３ぞくで２００えん　でございます。

_____ 4. *Sakki wa bikkuri shita naa. Amari odokasanai de kure yo.*
さっきは　びっくりしたなあ。あまり　おどかさないでくれよ。

_____ 5. *Ooi! Minna kocchi e koi yo.*
オーイ！みんな　こっちへこいよ。

_____ 6. *Piitaa san nihongo ga hontoo ni joozu ni narimashita ne.*
ピーターさん　にほんごが　ほんとうに　じょうずになりましたね。

_____ 7. *Dooshita no kashira? Takashi chan osoi wa ne.*
どうしたのかしら。たかしちゃん　おそいわね。

_____ 8. *Shinkansen wa yappari hayai naa. 2jikan de tsuichatta zo.*
しんかんせんは　やっぱり　はやいなあ。２じかんで　ついちゃったぞ。

_____ 9. *Doozo yukkuri omeshi agari kudasai.*
どうぞ　ゆっくり　おめしあがりください。

_____ 10. *Choodo yokatta wa. Watashi mo ie ni kaeru tokoro datta no.*
ちょうどよかったわ。わたしも　いえにかえるところだったの。

_____ 11. *Watashi mo Itaria ni ikoo kashira.*
わたしも　イタリアに　いこうかしら。

_____ 12. *Boku wa konban gaishoku shitai to omoimasu.*
ぼくは　こんばん　がいしょくしたい　とおもいます。

_____ 13. *Shachoo wa ima dekakete orimasu.*
しゃちょうは　いま　でかけております。

_____ 14. *Kondo no tesuto wa yasashii n datte.*
こんどのテストは　やさしいんだって。

LESSON 15

年	月	日
	曜日	番
名前		

(A) Fill in the blank spaces of the following verb conjugation chart. The verbs are from Lessons 10 11, 13, and 14 as well as from Volume One.

#	Dictionary Form	*-ba* Form	Passive Form	English: (*-ba*) (subject = "you")
1		*migakeba*		
2	*furu*			
3				if you wear shoes
4			*hajimerareru*	
5	*hanasu*			
6				if you forget
7			*iwareru*	
8		*kaereba*		
9				if you write
10	*kau*			
11				if you wear
12	*kuru*			
13		*tsutaereba*		
14			*norareru*	
15				if you remember
16	*oshieru*			
17		*sagaseba*		
18				if you do
19			*taberareru*	
20	*toru*			

年	月	日
	曜日	番
名前		

B) Using the phonetic sounds in each set, try to make as many words as possible from Volume One and Volume Two.

Example: mi   no   shi   ta   no
_____*mita*;   *shita*;   *tanoshimi*_____

1. i   u   ka   ta   shi   ma

_____   _____   _____

_____   _____   _____

_____   _____   _____

2. ka   ta   ha   mi   chi   na

_____   _____   _____

_____   _____   _____

_____   _____   _____

	年	月	日
		曜日	番
名前			

(C) Change the following statements into questions using *-masen deshita ka?* Follow the example.

Example: *Yuube watashi ni denwa shita.*   ゆうべ　わたしにでんわした。

　　　　Yuube watashi ni denwa shimasen deshita ka?   ゆうべ　わたしにでんわしませんでしたか。

1. *Watashi no tsukue no hikidashi* (drawer) *o aketa.* わたしの　つくえの　ひきだしをあけた。

　　_____

2. *Watashi ga inai toki Piitaa ga kita.*   わたしがいないとき　ピーターがきた。

　　_____

3. *Sono tegami o nihongo de kaita.*   そのてがみを　にほんごでかいた。

　　_____

4. *Omiyage no chokoreeto o tabeta.*   おみやげのチョコレートをたべた。

　　_____

5. *Jugyoo no beru ga natta* (naru).   じゅぎょうのベルがなった。

　　_____

6. *Watashi ni tegami ga todoita.*   わたしに　てがみがとどいた。

　　_____

7. *Daidokoro de kuruma no kagi o mita.*   だいどころで　くるまのかぎをみた。

　　_____

LESSON 15

年	月	日
	曜日	番
名前		

D) Following the example, translate the following Japanese sentences into English.

Example: *Kyooto e wa itta hoo ga ii desu yo.*　きょうとへは　いったほうがいいですよ。
<u>You should go to Kyoto.</u> OR <u>It would be better if you go to Kyoto.</u>

1. *Gozenchuu wa ikanai hoo ga ii desu yo.*　ごぜんちゅうは　いかないほうがいいですよ。

_____

2. *Akai hoo ga suki desu.*　あかいほうがすきです。

_____

3. *Amari yawarakakunai hoo ga ii desu.*　あまりやわらかくないほうがいいです。

_____

4. *Reezaa purintaa o tsukawanai hoo ga ii desu.*　レーザープリンターを　つかわないほうがいいです。

_____

5. *Moo sukoshi osoi jikan no hoo ga ii n desu ga.*　もうすこし　おそいじかんのほうがいいんですが。

_____

6. *Gureepu furuutsu yori orenji no hoo ga suki desu.*
グレープフルーツより　オレンジのほうがすきです。

_____

7. *Enryo shinai hoo ga ii desu yo.*　えんりょしないほうがいいですよ。

_____

8. *Chikatetsu ni noru hoo ga ii desu yo.*　ちかてつにのるほうがいいですよ。

_____

9. *Tabete iru toki wa, hanasanai hoo ga ii desu yo.*
たべているときは、はなさないほうがいいですよ。

_____

LESSON 16

(A) Find and circle the Japanese equivalent of the 12 English words from Lesson 16 that are liste
below. They are written horizontally, vertically, diagonally, and backwards.

N	E	N	G	O	P	W	J	S	T	Y	M
I	E	T	I	H	S	A	M	E	K	A	O
H	T	N	J	R	K	G	A	N	A	M	K
A	E	T	N	U	D	E	R	I	S	U	O
S	B	M	A	I	S	H	H	O	H	Z	T
A	A	E	K	A	H	S	U	O	I	U	O
R	R	B	P	O	I	S	N	J	T	K	S
A	I	K	A	N	T	A	A	A	E	A	H
D	H	E	U	S	T	R	S	G	U	S	I
R	S	U	I	N	Y	U	O	N	N	H	N
I	J	I	A	A	K	R	P	E	J	I	O
E	T	K	O	H	S	I	J	N	A	I	K

1. "open"
2. dictionary
3. this year

4. Chinese characters
5. simple
6. difficult

7. lend
8. "Happy New Year"
9. check

10. New Year's car
11. monkey
12. Chinese calenda

	年	月	日
	曜日		番
名前			

B) From the list of sentences in the box below, choose the one which best completes each of the following diaglogues and write the letter in the parenthesis.

1. A: *Kono doa oshite mo hiite mo akimasen.*　　　　B: (　　　)
　　このドア　おしてもひいても　あきません。

2. A: *Koko ni atta manjuu dare ka shiranai?*　　　　B: (　　　)
　　ここにあったまんじゅう　だれかしらない。

3. A: (　　　)　　　　B: *Oishisoo.*　　おいしそう。

4. A: (　　　)　　　　B: *Ii desu, ashita sanpatsu* (barber shop) *ni iku tsumori desu kara.*
　　　　　　　　　　　いいです、あした　さんぱつにいく　つもりですから。

5. A: (　　　)　　　　B: *Hayaku yonda n desu nee.*　　はやく　よんだんですねえ。

6. A: *Kyuu ni hashittara ashi ga itaku natchatta.*　　　　B: (　　　)
　　きゅうに　はしったら　あしがいたくなっちゃった。

7. A: (　　　)　　　　B: *Hontoo. Tasukaru wa. Arigatoo.*
　　　　　　　　　　　ほんとう。たすかるわ。ありがとう。

---

a. *Sono nimotsu omosoo da ne. Boku ga motte ageru yo.*
　そのにもつ　おもそうだね。ぼくが　もってあげるよ。

b. *Kami ga nagaku narimashita nee. Kitte agemashoo ka?*
　かみが　ながくなりましたねえ。きってあげましょうか。

c. *Suraido shite minasai. Soo sureba akimasu yo.*
　スライドしてみなさい。そうすれば　あきますよ。

d. *Senshuu karita hon futsuka de yonde shimaimashita.*
　せんしゅうかりたほん　ふつかで　よんでしまいました。

e. *Kore o hatte goran. Sugu naoru kara.*
　これをはってごらん。すぐ　なおるから。

f. *Te o dashite goran. Ojiichan ga Ken chan no suki na chokoreeto katte kita yo.*
　てをだしてごらん。おじいちゃんが　けんちゃんのすきなチョコレート　かってきたよ。

g. *Are anata no datta no? Gomen nasai. Watashi ga tabete shimaimashita.*
　あれ　あなたのだったの。ごめんなさい。わたしが　たべてしまいました。

LESSON 16

(C) Complete the following sentences by choosing the most appropriate English verb listed below. In the blank, write the Japanese equivalent in its *-te* form.

1. *Kasa o koko ni _____ ii desu ka?*

   かさを　ここに＿＿＿＿＿＿＿＿いいですか。

2. *Kyoo wa Nanshii san ga kuruma de _____ kuremashita.*

   きょうは　ナンシーさんが　くるまで＿＿＿＿＿＿＿くれました。

3. *Asoko de tabako o _____ iru hito wa dare desu ka?*

   あそこで　たばこを＿＿＿＿＿＿＿いるひとは　だれですか。

4. *Watashi ga tegami o _____ agemasu.*

   わたしが　てがみを＿＿＿＿＿＿＿あげます。

5. *Saishuu no basu wa moo _____ shimaimashita.*

   さいしゅうのバスは　もう＿＿＿＿＿＿＿しまいました。

6. *Kinoo made _____ imashita ga, _____ shimaimashita.*

   きのうまで＿＿＿＿＿＿＿いましたが、＿＿＿＿＿＿＿しまいました。

7. *Kochira ga watashi no inakunatta koinu o _____ kureta hito desu.*

   こちらが　わたしの　いなくなったこいぬを＿＿＿＿＿＿＿くれたひとです。

8. *Ima _____ iru no wa dochira no chiimu desu ka?*

   いま＿＿＿＿＿＿＿いるのは　どちらのチームですか。

find	forget	leave	put	remember	send	smoke	win	write

64

A) Create your own original sentences using the given words. Verbs may be used in any tense, and the given words may be used in any order. Try to make sentences that are different from the Sample Conversation.

1. *tera* てら, *jinja* じんじゃ, *toshi* とし _____

_____

2. *shizen* しぜん, *basho* ばしょ _____

_____

3. *hidari no* ひだりの, *migi no* みぎの _____

_____

4. *inoru* いのる, *sosen* そせん _____

_____

5. *omairi* おまいり, *ichinen* いちねん _____

_____

6. *oshoogatsu* おしょうがつ, *kakunin suru* かくにんする _____

_____

7. *rei* れい, *tame ni* ために _____

_____

8. *fushigi* ふしぎ, *fuukei* ふうけい _____

_____

LESSON 17

(B) Complete the following sentences by matching each one with the most appropriate phrase from the box below. Conjugate the verb in the second phrase accordingly.

1. *"Obon" ni tsuite shiraberu tame*　　おぼんについて　しらべるため

_____

2. *Asa no kaigi ni shusseki suru tame*　　あさのかいぎに　しゅっせきするため

_____

3. *Nihongo ga joozu ni hanaseru yoo ni naru tame*　　にほんごが　じょうずにはなせるようになるため

_____

4. *Jisaboke ni naranai yoo ni suru tame*　　じさぼけにならないように するため

_____

5. *Shuumatsu tomodachi to asobu tame*　　しゅうまつ　ともだちとあそぶため

_____

6. *Akiko wa kukkii o tsukuru tame*　　あきこは　クッキーをつくるため

_____

7. *Hiroshi wa sakkaa no senshu ni naru tame*　　ひろしは　サッカーのせんしゅになるため

_____

> *Burajiru ni ryuugaku suru*　　ブラジルに　りゅうがくする
> *hikooki no naka de shikkari neru*　　ひこうきのなかで　しっかりねる
> *kesa wa ie o hayaku deru*　　けさは　いえをはやくでる
> *kyoojuu ni shukudai o katazukeru*　　きょうじゅうに　しゅくだいをかたずける
> *mainichi renshuu suru*　　まいにち　れんしゅうする
> *okaasan ni tsukurikata o manabu*　　おかあさんに　つくりかたをまなぶ
> *toshokan e iku*　　としょかんへ　いく

年	月	日
	曜日	番
名前		

C) Complete the following dialogues by writing a question for Part A based on Part B's answer. Be sure to use the form *Moo --- mo ii desu ka?* Follow the example.

Example: A: *Moo tabete mo ii desu ka?*   もう　たべてもいいですか。
 B: *Hai, tabete kudasai.*   はい、たべてください。

1. A: _____

 B: *Moo sukoshi tatte ite kudasai.*   もうすこし　たっていてください。

2. A: _____

 B: *Beru ga naru made hajimenai de kudasai.*   ベルがなるまで　はじめないでください。

3. A: _____

 B: *Naze yameru n desu ka?*   なぜ　やめるんですか。

4. A: _____

 B: *Mada 9ji desu yo. Neru ni wa hayasugimasu.*   まだ　9じですよ。ねるには　はやすぎます。

5. A: _____

 B: *Mada kaette wa ikemasen.*   まだ　かえってはいけません。

6. A: _____

 B: *Hai, keshite mo ii desu.*   はい、けしてもいいです。

(D) This exercise practices the use of counting animate and inanimate objects. Translate the following into Japanese. Be sure to use the correct counter suffix.

	English	*Nihongo*
1	one person	
2	one item	
3	two days	
4	two pieces of paper	
5	three people	
6	three small boxes	
7	four days	
8	four books	
9	five months	
10	five cars	
11	six pens	
12	six items	
13	seven people	
14	seven pieces of paper	
15	eight days	
16	eight months	
17	nine items	
18	nine pencils	
19	ten days	
20	ten small boxes	

	年	月	日
	曜日		番
名前			

A) The words listed in the box below are from Lessons 11 through 17. Group them into 7 different categories according to the given topic or hint. The number of blanks signifies the number of words that must be added to each group. Some words are listed to give you a hint for each category.

1. New Year: _____sarudoshi_____   _____nengajoo_____   _____

     _____   _____   _____

2. temples &   _____sosen_____   _____jinja_____   _____
   shrines:

     _____   _____   _____

3. weather: _____hare_____   _____   _____

     _____

4. adverbs: _____hajimete_____   _____chikaku_____   _____

     _____   _____   _____

5. adjectives: _____furui_____   _____   _____

     _____   _____   _____

6. expressions: _____soryaa_____   _____yappari_____   _____

     _____   _____

7. nouns: _____kotoshi_____   _____daitokai_____   _____

     _____   _____   _____

---

akemashite omedetoo,   ame,   atarashii,   atto iu ma,   chikai,   denkiseihin,
futte imasu,   gaikokujin,   gurai,   ichinen,   inorimasu,   juunishi,   kingashinnen,
muzukashii,   nagusameru,   no naka ni,   no soto ni,   ohakamairi,   ooi,
oshoogatsu,   rei,   seinoo,   shimatta,   tenkiyohoo,   tonikaku,   yasui,   zettai

LESSON 18

(B) Each of the following contains two sentences. Read both sentences carefully in order to get the meaning. Choose the correct verb from the list below, conjugate it, and fill in the blank of the first sentence. Follow the example. Not all of the verbs are used.

Example: *Kono tegami o dashitai no desu. Kono chikaku ni posuto wa arimasen ka?*
このてがみを　だしたいのです。このちかくに　ポストはありませんか。

1. *Tsumetai ocha o _____. Arimasu ka?*
   つめたいおちゃを_____。ありますか。

2. *Eiji shinbun o _____. Soko no Japan Taimuzu o totte kuremasen ka?*
   えいじしんぶんを_____。そこのジャパンタイムズを　とってくれませんか。

3. *Ueno de _____. Kono densha wa Ueno de tomarimasu ka?*
   うえので_____。このでんしゃは　うえのでとまりますか。

4. *Okinawa e _____. Tookyoo kara tonde iru hikooki gaisha o shitte imasu ka?*
   おきなわへ_____。とうきょうからとんでいる　ひこうきがいしゃを　しっていますか。

5. *Nihon no karendaa o _____. Nihon no mono o utte iru omise o shirimasen ka?*
   にほんのカレンダーを_____。にほんのものを　うっているおみせを　しりませんか。

6. *Sukii ni _____. Dono sukiijoo ga ii desu ka?*
   スキーに_____。どのスキーじょうが　いいですか。

7. *Piza o _____. Dono omise ga oishii desu ka?*
   ピザを_____。どのおみせが　おいしいですか。

---

aruku あるく, *dasu* だす, *iku* いく, *kaku* かく, *kau* かう, *kuru* くる, *nomu* のむ, *noru* のる, *oriru* おりる, *ryokoo suru* りょこうする, *taberu* たべる, *tsukuru* つくる, *yobu* よぶ, *yomu* よむ

70

C) Complete the following sentences by conjugating the verb in parentheses into the potential (can/capable) form. Then translate the sentence into English. For some sentences, the verbs may be either positive or negative; for others there is only one choice. Follow the example.

Example: *Tanoshikatta nihonryokoo no koto ga (wasureraremasen).*   *[wasureru]*
      たのしかった　にほんりょこうのことが（わすれられません）。
      <u>I cannot forget the enjoyable trip to Japan.</u>

1. *Sono pan mada (*   *) ka?* *[taberu]*
   そのパン　まだ（　　　　　　　　）か？　「たべる」
   _____

2. *Ashita no asa 6ji ni (*   *) to omoimasu.* *[okiru]*
   あしたのあさ６じに（　　　　　　　）とおもいます。　「おきる」
   _____

3. *Yuube wa mushiatsukute (*   *) deshita.* *[neru]*
   ゆうべは　むしあつくて（　　　　　　　）でした。　「ねる」
   _____

4. *Sore wa himitsu dakara (*   *).* *[oshieru]*
   それは　ひみつだから（　　　　　　　）。　「おしえる」
   _____

5. *Kanojo wa ima taihen isogashikute (*   *) soo desu.* *[kuru]*
   かのじょは　いま　たいへんいそがしくて（　　　　　）そうです。　「くる」
   _____

6. *Kono hon (*   *) ka?* *[kariru]*
   このほん（　　　　　　）か。　「かりる」
   _____

7. *Ji ga taihen chiisai desu ga (*   *) ka?* *[yomu]*
   じが　たいへんちいさいですが（　　　　　）か。　「よむ」
   _____

8. *Ashi o nenza* (sprain) *shite ite mo (*   *) ka?* *[aruku]*
   あしを　ねんざしていても（　　　　　）か。　「あるく」
   _____

LESSON 18

	年	月	日
	曜日		番
名前			

(D) Match the phrases in Group A with the correct phrase from Group B. Write the letter in the space provided.

GROUP A

1. *Kyoo wa samui kara,* (   ). きょうは　さむいから、

2. *Kyoo wa atsui kara,* (   ). きょうは　あついから、

3. *Kyoo wa oomisoka* (New Year's Eve) *dakara,* (   ). きょうは　おおみそかだから、

4. *Konban wa futari dake dakara,* (   ). こんばんは　ふたりだけだから、

5. *Kyoo wa natsubate* (tired due to hot, humid weather) *ni naranai yoo ni,* (   ).
   きょうは　なつバテにならないように、

6. *Kyoo wa Haruko ga daigaku ni gookaku shita* (got accepted) *kara,* (   ).
   きょうは　はるこが　だいがくにごうかくしたから、

7. *Keeki o katte kita kara,* (   ). ケーキを　かってきたから、

8. *Ashita wa ohigan* (the equinox) *dakara,* (   ). あしたは　おひがんだから、

9. *Hikkoshi* (moving) *mo owattashi,* (   ). ひっこしも　おわったし、

10. *Ashita wa Yuuji no gakkoo no undookai dakara,* (   ).
    あしたは　ゆうじのがっこうの　うんどうかいだから、

GROUP B

a. *ohagi* (rice dumpling with bean paste) *o katte kimasu.* おはぎを　かってきます。

b. *onigiri o tsukuroo ka?* おにぎりを　つくろうか。

c. *sorosoro hikkoshisoba* (a type of thick noodles) *o tabeyoo ka?*
   そろそろひっこしそばをたべようか。

d. *3ji no oyatsu* (snack) *ni tabemashoo.* ３じのおやつに　たべましょう。

e. *toshikoshisoba* (a type of thick noodles) *o tabe nakya.* としこしそばを　たべなきゃ。

f. *naberyoori* (various vegetables and meat boiled together) *ni shimashoo ka?*
   なべりょうりに　しましょうか。

g. *gaishoku* (eating out) *ni shimashoo?* がいしょくに　しましょう。

h. *chuushoku wa soomen* (cold, thin noodles) *ni shimashoo ka?*
   ちゅうしょくは　そうめんにしましょうか。

i. *unagi* (eel) *ni shimashoo ka?* うなぎに　しましょうか。

j. *osekihan* (rice cooked with red beans) *o taite iwaimashoo.*
   おせきはんを　たいて　いわいましょう。

72

A) Complete the following sentences with words or phrases from Lesson 19.

1. *Kirisutokyoo ga watashi no ie no* _____ *desu.*

   キリストきょうが　わたしのいえの_____です。

2. _____ *wa Taiwan no* _____ *ni arimasu.*

   _____はたいわんの_____にあります。

3. *Anata no* _____ *wa Toyota desu ne. Sono kuruma wa*_____

   desu ka?

   あなたの_____はトヨタですね。そのくるまは_____ですか。

4. *Chuugoku ya* _____ *de wa taberu toki* _____ *o*

   tsukaimasu.

   ちゅうごくや_____ではたべるとき_____をつかいます。

5. *Nihon to Chuugoku to Kankoku wa* _____ _____ *ni arimasu.*

   にほんと　ちゅうごくと　かんこくは_____ _____にあります。

6. *Hotondo no nihonjin wa* _____ *ka shintoo to iu shuukyoo o shinjite* (believe)

   iru rashii desu yo.

   ほとんどのにほんじんは_____か　しんとうというしゅうきょうを　しんじているらしいですよ。

7. *Taiwan ni itta toki ni* _____ *o tabemashita ka? Oishikatta desu ka?*

   たいわんにいったときに_____をたべましたか。おいしかったですか。

8. *Ajia de ichiban ooki na* _____ *wa dore desu ka?*

   アジアでいちばんおおきな_____はどれですか。

(B) Complete the following sentences by filling in the blanks. The target expression for this exercise is --- *to ieba* --- *desu.* Follow the example.

Example: *Nyuu Yooku to ieba <u>jiyuu no megami</u> desu.*   ニューヨークといえば　<u>じゆうのめがみ</u>です。

1. *Nihon to ieba* _____ *desu.*   にほんといえば_____です。

2. _____ *to ieba Yooroppa desu.*   _____といえば　ヨーロッパです。

3. *Pari to ieba* _____ *desu.*   パリといえば_____です。

4. *Wain to ieba* _____ *desu.*   ワインといえば_____です。

5. *Nihonryoori to ieba* _____ *desu.*   にほんりょうりといえば_____です。

6. _____ *to ieba* _____ *desu.*

7. _____ *to ieba* _____ *desu.*

8. _____ *to ieba* _____ *desu.*

9. _____ *to ieba* _____ *desu.*

10. _____ *to ieba* _____ *desu.*

C) Answer the following questions using the expression --- *toka* --- *toka*. Follow the example.
You may need to consult with your teacher or reference books to answer some of the questions.

Example: *Osushi no gohan ni wa donna choomiryoo* (seasoning) *o iremasu ka?*
おすしのごはんには　どんなちょうみりょうを　いれますか。
Satoo toka osu toka o iremasu.　さとうとか　おすとか　をいれます。

1. *Sukiyaki ni wa donna yasai o iremasu ka?*　すきやきには　どんなやさいを　いれますか

_____ *o iremasu.*

2. *Amerika no kookoo de wa donna kyooka o benkyoo shimasu ka?*
アメリカのこうこうでは　どんなきょうかを　べんきょうしますか。

_____ *mo benkyoo shimasu.*

3. *Amerika ni wa donna jidoosha meekaa ga arimasu ka?*
アメリカには　どんなじどうしゃメーカーが　ありますか。

_____ *nado ga ariamsu.*

4. *Nihon ni wa donna pasuta ga arimasu ka?*　にほんには　どんなパスタが　ありますか。

_____ *nado ga arimasu.*

5. *Amerika no yuumei na basukettobooru senshu wa dare desu ka?*
アメリカの　ゆうめいな　バスケットボールせんしゅは　だれですか。

_____

soshite hoka ni mo yuumei na senshu ga takusan imasu.

6. *Nihon yori hiroi Amerika no shuu wa dore desu ka?*
にほんよりひろい　アメリカのしゅうは　どれですか。

_____ *desu.*

7. *Amerika ni wa donna faasuto foodo ga arimsu ka?*
アメリカには　どんなファーストフードが　ありますか。

_____ *nado ga arimasu.*

LESSON 20

年	月	日
	曜日	番
名前		

(A) Translate the following English words into Japanese and the Japanese words into English. Most of them are from Lesson 20; others are from Volume One.

	English	*Nihongo*
1	Valentine's Day	
2	duty	
3	middle of the night	
4	look sleepy	
5	did not sleep	
6	talked	
7	brown	
8	entrance	
9	rabbit	
10	culture	
11		*kuwashiku*
12		*okutta*
13		*nijukko*
14		*kazu*
15		*oshiete*
16		*nesshin ni*
17		*semai*
18		*taitei*
19		*sakubun*
20		*yoofuku*

	年	月	日
		曜日	番
名前			

(B) Using the expression -*soo*, complete the following sentences by describing each of the situations. Follow the example.

Example: You are talking to your friend who seems sleepy. You say ...

     Nani ka nemusoo ne.   なにか　ねむそうね。

1. A boy walks up to a group of his classmates who seem to be having a good time and says ...

    _____ *da naa.*

2. A friend of yours seems worried about something. Wondering what it is, you ask ...

    Sonna ni _____ *o shite dooshita no?*

3. A girl finds a kitten (*koneko*) stranded on the side of the road and says to herself ...

    Maa, _____ .

4. At an auto show you see a lot of fancy cars, such as Lamborghinis and Ferraris. You say ...

    Totemo _____ *da na.*

5. You and your classmate want to talk to your teacher, but he/she seems to be in the middle of an important meeting. You say ...

    Nani ka _____ *mitai yo.*

6. You are looking at the dark clouds in the sky. You say ...

    Nani ka _____ *ne.*

7. Watching the final round of a sumo tournament on TV, you see that one wrestler has defeated all of his opponents. You say ...

    Totemo _____ *da ne.*

	年	月	日
		曜日	番
名前			

(C) Using the epxression *nani o sonna ni*, fill in the blanks to complete each of the following dialogues. Follow the example.

Example: A: *Yuube osoku made tomodachi to denwa de hanashichatta.*
ゆうべおそくまで　ともだちと　でんわではなしちゃった。

B: *Nani o sonna ni osoku made hanashita no?*　なにをそんなに　おそくまで　はなしたの。

A: *Barentain choko ni tsuite hanashita no.*　バレンタインチョコについて　はなしたの。

1. A: *Kono shoppingu baggu hitotsu motte kure yo. Totemo omoi n da.*
このショッピングバッグひとつ　もってくれよ。とても　おもいんだ。

B: _____ ?

A: *Koora 20pon mo katta n da yo.*
コーラ２０ぽんも　かったんだよ。

2. A: *Kondo no nihongo sakubun wa 10peeji mo kaichatta.*
こんどの　にほんごさくぶんは　１０ページもかいちゃった。

B: _____ ?

A: *Nihonryokoo no omoide yo.*　にほんりょこうの　おもいでよ。

3. A: *Mite, mite! Tomodachi ni konna ni takusan hon o karichatta yo.*
みて、みて！ともだちに　こんなにたくさん　ほんをかりちゃったよ。

B: _____ ?

A: *Manga yo.*　マンガよ。

4. A: *Aaa benkyoo shisugite, atama ga itai yo.*　あああ　べんきょうしすぎて、あたまがいたいよ。

B: _____ ?

A: *Boku no kirai na suugaku nan da.*　ぼくのきらいな　すうがくなんだ。

5. A: *Shinpai da naa.*　しんぱいだなあ。

B: _____ ?

A: *Nihongo kurasu no seiseki no koto.*　にほんごクラスの　せいせきのこと。

LESSON 21

<table>
<tr><td></td><td>年</td><td>月</td><td>日</td></tr>
<tr><td></td><td>曜日</td><td></td><td>番</td></tr>
<tr><td>名前</td><td></td><td></td><td></td></tr>
</table>

(A) Fill in the blank spaces of the following verb conjugation chart. The verbs are from Lessons 16, 17, 19, and 20 as well as from Volume One.

#	Dictionary Form	Pre -*masu* + *masen*	Potential (can/capable) Form	English: potential
1		*akemasen*		
2				can wash
3		*hairimasen*		
4			*hanaseru*	
5				can pay
6				can go
7			*inoreru*	
8	*ireru*			
9				can say, can tell
10			*keseru*	
11				can decide
12	*nagusameru*			
13		*nemasen*		
14	*oboeru*			
15	*okuru*			
16	*oshieru*			
17		*shimasen*		
18	*taberu*			
19				can use
20			*ureru*	

79

<table>
<tr><td colspan="2">年　　　　月　　　　日</td></tr>
<tr><td colspan="2">曜日　　　　　　番</td></tr>
<tr><td>名前</td><td></td></tr>
</table>

(B) Complete the following crossword puzzle. Words and clues are taken mostly from Lessons 7 and 8. All answers are in Japanese. For English clues in quotations, the answer is the Japanese translation.

ACROSS

1. February 14
6. "made in Korea"
8. "number"
9. uncooked rice
10. done at *tera* or *jinja*
11. "to say"
12. *kyonen* _____ *rainen*
14. *chuugokugo no ji*
16. *Kambojia, Tai, Betonamu wa* _____ *Ajia ni arimasu.*
18. *nezumi, ushi, tora, usagi ...*
19. "anything else"

DOWN

1. *Nihon no shuukyoo no hitotsu*
2. _____ *kara nemui yo.*
3. "Do not hesitate."
4. "scene"
5. *Nihonryoori ni hashi o* _____.
7. "shopping"
13. "three"
15. *Tango ga wakaranai toki* _____ *o tsukau.*
17. *Nihon to Chuugoku to Taiwan to Kankoku wa* _____ *ni arimasu.*

(C) The following dialogues begin with one of the three questions in the box below. In the space provided, write the letter of the most appropriate one.

1. A: (　　)

   B: *Udon ya soba mo arimasu.*　　うどんや　そばも　あります。

2. A: (　　)

   B: *Boku mo sanka shimasu.*　　ぼくも　さんかします。

3. A: (　　)

   B: *Pikunikku ya haikingu mo ii to omoimasu.* ピクニックや　ハイキングも　いいとおもいます。

4. A: (　　)

   B: *Yosemite Kooen toka Taho Ko ga ii to omoimasu ga, doo deshoo?*
   ヨセミテこうえんとか　タホこが　いいとおもいますが、どうでしょう。

5. A: (　　)

   B: *Kyooto ya Nara mo ii desu yo.*　　きょうとや　ならも　いいですよ。

6. A: (　　)

   B: *A, Joodan ya Oniiru nado ga imasu yo.*　あ、ジョーダンや　オニールなどが　いますよ。

7. A: (　　)

   B: *"Ka" o tsukenai de gimonbun ni suru hoohoo ni tsuite oshiete kudasai.*
   「か」をつけないで　ぎもんぶんにする　ほうほうについて　おしえてください。

8. A: (　　)

   B: *Terebi no ushiro toka kurozetto no ura wa doo desu ka?*
   テレビのうしろとか　クロゼットのうらは　どうですか。

a. *Hoka ni nani ka arimasen ka?*　　ほかに　なにかありませんか。
b. *Hoka ni dare ka imasen ka?*　　ほかに　だれかいませんか。
c. *Hoka ni doko ka arimasen ka?*　　ほかに　どこかありませんか。

LESSON 21

曜日　番

名前

(D) Complete the following sentences by filling in the blanks with one of the words or expressions written in the box below. Some may be used more than once, and others may not be used at all.

1. _____ *kare ga yuushoo suru to wa omowanakatta na.*

   _____かれが　ゆうしょうするとは　おもわなかったな。

2. _____ *kare mo kotoshi de 27sai ni natta n da ne.*

   _____かれも　ことしで　２７さいになったんだね。

3. _____ *mata ashita.* _____また　あした。

4. _____ ... *sumimasen omoidasemasen.* _____...すみません　おもいだせません。

5. *Tabun soo iu koto* _____.　　たぶん　そういうこと_____。

6. _____ ...*watashi wa shirimasen.* _____...わたしは　しりません。

7. _____ *sonna koto wa nai to omoimasu yo.*

   _____そんなことはない　とおもいますよ。

8. _____ *watashi mo minna to issho ni itte ii to iu koto?*

   _____わたしも　みんなといっしょにいっていい　ということ。

9. *Sore tte Nanshii no koto?* _____ *Nanshii kondo no natsu Nihon ni iku n datte*

   それって　ナンシーのこと。 _____ナンシー　こんどのなつ　にほんにいくんだって。

10. _____ *kore? Motto Nihon rashii omiyage nakatta no?*

    _____これ。もっと　にほんらしいおみやげ　なかったの

---

deshoo (ne) でしょう（ね）, *E* え, *Ee* ええ, *Eeto* ええと, *Ja* じゃ,
Masaka まさか, *Nani* なに, *Saa* さあ, *Soo ieba* そういえば,

年	月	日
	曜日	番
名前		

(A) Categorize the words listed below into the chart based on the given topics. Some words may belong to more than one topic.

Ie いえ	
Gakkoo がっこう	
Ryokoo りょこう	
Mooru モール	
Resutoran レストラン	

amutorakku アムトラック, *bangohan* ばんごはん, *benkyoo jikan* べんきょうじかん, *Berugii* ベルギー, *burausu* ブラウス, *chika* ちか, *chippu* チップ, *chooshoku* ちょうしょく, *daidokoro* だいどころ, *denkiseihin* でんきせいひん, *densha* でんしゃ, *depaato* デパート, *Doitsu* ドイツ, *ehagaki* えはがき, *eiga* えいが, *fasshon* ファッション, *fune* ふね, *gaikokujin* がいこくじん, *gaishoku* がいしょく, *ha o migaku* はをみがく, *heya* へや, *hikooki* ひこうき, *hiruyasumi* ひるやすみ, *hoteru* ホテル, *Igirisu* イギリス, *imushitsu* いむしつ, *itariaryoori* イタリアりょうり, *jisaboke* じさボケ, *jugyoo* じゅぎょう, *kafeteria* カフェテリア, *kaimono* かいもの, *kameraya* カメラや, *Kankoku* かんこく, *kateika* かていか, *kazoku* かぞく, *kimatsushiken* きまつしけん, *kippu* きっぷ, *kokusaikuukoo* こくさいくうこう, *koochoo sensei* こうちょうせんせい, *kyoodai* きょうだい, *kyookasho* きょうかしょ, *Makudonarudo* マクドナルド, *menyuu* メニュー, *nyuugakushiken* にゅうがくしけん, *omiyage* おみやげ, *oshibori* おしぼり, *rekishi* れきし, *seetaa* セーター, *sotsugyooshiki* そつぎょうしき, *sukaato* スカート, *suugaku* すうがく, *taiikukan* たいいくかん, *terebi* テレビ, *uchi* うち, *ueitoresu* ウェートレス, *yoofuku* ようふく, *yoyaku* よやく, *zubon* ズボン

(B) The expressions --- *mitai* and --- *rashii* have several different meanings, depending on how they are used. Three of these meanings are listed below. Choose the correct meaning of the underlined part of each sentence and write the letter in the parentheses. Then translate the sentences into English.

(a) want to (try)　　　(b) looks/seems (like)　　　(c) typical of

1. *Onaka ga suite iru mitai.*　(　　　)　おなかがすいている　みたい。(　　　)

　　_____

2. *Watashi mo sushi o tabete mitai naa.*　(　　　)　わたしも　すしをたべてみたいなあ。(　　　)

　　_____

3. *Ano hitotachi wa konsaato no kippu o kau tame ni narande iru rashii no.*　(　　　)
　　あのひとたちは　コンサートのきっぷをかうために　ならんでいるらしいの。(　　　)

　　_____

4. *Anata mo shamisen no oto o kiite mitai desu ka?*　(　　　)
　　あなたも　しゃみせんのおとを　きいてみたいですか。(　　　)

　　_____

5. *Kyoo wa getsuyoobi rashii getsuyoobi ne.*　(　　　)　きょうは　げつようびらしい　げつようびね。(

　　_____

6. *Zehi kotoshijuu ni itte mitai desu.*　(　　　)　ぜひ　ことしじゅうに　いってみたいです。(

　　_____

7. *Yamada sensei, gakusei rashii fuku tte donna fuku desu ka?*　(　　　)
　　やまだせんせい、がくせいらしいふくって　どんなふくですか。(　　　)

　　_____

8. *Kono tori wa kega o shite iru mitai.*　(　　　)　このとりは　けがをしているみたい。(　　　)

　　_____

9. *Ano kazoku wa Tekisasujin rashii hanashikata o suru ne.*　(　　　)
　　あのかぞくは　テキサス人らしい　はなしかたをするね。(　　　)

　　_____

10. *Piitaa mo onaji uookuman o katta mitai yo.*　(　　　)
　　ピーターも　おなじウォークマンを　かったみたいよ。(　　　)

　　_____

年	月	日
	曜日	番
名前		

C) Translate the following sentences into Japanese. Be sure to use verbs in the causative form.
   (e.g. *kaku* → *kakaseru*)

1. The mother made her child swim by himself.

   _____

2. His father made him practice the piano for three hours every day.

   _____

3. Please don't make him drink alcohol.

   _____

4. Please don't make her go by herself.

   _____

5. Our Japanese teacher makes us memorize five new words every day.

   _____

6. The teacher made the students wait outside for half an hour.

   _____

7. The police officer made everyone drive slowly on the snowy road.

   _____

8. Why did your father make you give up tennis?

   _____

LESSON 23

(A) Unscramble the following words. The first 10 are from Lesson 23; the others are from Volume One. The first letter of each word is given to help you. Words are in the same form as in the Sample Conversation and in the Vocabulary List.

1. neznan	→	z _____
2. euhnss	→	s _____
3. pihnias	→	s _____
4. uhstimius	→	i _____
5. euoktsss	→	k _____
6. nakat	→	t _____
7. naezn	→	n _____
8. suukmesazut	→	t _____
9. aaiink	→	i _____
10. ifeurri	→	r _____
11. ossuikh	→	s _____
12. utisteas	→	t _____
13. hnojniin	→	n _____
14. ydokiao	→	k _____
15. nisnmaa	→	m _____
16. ipnuest	→	e _____
17. gshhiai	→	h _____
18. kraiau	→	a _____
19. okukoby	→	b _____
20. hnhsiaa	→	h _____

	年	月	日
	曜日		番
名前			

B) Create a two-line dialogue using --- *e ikanai* or --- *e ikimashoo* as well as the words given for each problem. Follow the example.

Example: *Kondo no nichiyoobi ----- eiga*　　　こんどのにちようび-----えいが
  A: <u>*Kondo no nichiyoobi eiga e ikanai?*</u>　こんどのにちようび　えいがへいかない。
  B: <u>*Ii kedo akushon eiga wa iya da yo.*</u>　いいけど　アクションえいがは　いやだよ。

1. *raishuu no nichiyoobi ----- konsaato*　　らいしゅうのにちようび-----コンサート
  A: _____
  B: _____

2. *gakkoo no kaerimichi ----- toshokan*　　がっこうのかえりみち-----としょかん
  A: _____
  B: _____

3. *konshuu no doyoobi ----- sakanatsuri*　　こんしゅうのどようび-----さかなつり
  A: _____
  B: _____

4. *rainen no natsu ----- nihongo kyanpu*　　らいねんのなつ-----にほんごキャンプ
  A: _____
  B: _____

5. *ima kara ----- kissaten*　　いまから-----きっさてん
  A: _____
  B: _____

6. *gogo kara----- dauntaun*　　ごごから-----ダウンタウン
  A: _____
  B: _____

年		月		日
		曜日		番
名前				

(C) Each of the following sentences has one grammatical mistake. Circle the mistake and rewrite the entire sentence.

1. *Kondo no eiga ga tabun omoshirokunai daroo to omoimasu.*
   こんどのえいがが　たぶんおもしろくないだろう　とおもいます。

   _____

2. *Watashi no hanashi wa wakaranai toki wa te o agete kudasai.*
   わたしのはなしは　わからないときは　てをあげてください。

   _____

3. *Sore o sensei ni tsutaeru no wa wasurete imashita.*
   それを　せんせいにつたえるのは　わすれていました。

   _____

4. *Shinsetsu na ojisan ga obaachan o ie made okutte moraimashita.*
   しんせつなおじさんが　おばあちゃんを　いえまでおくってもらいました。

   _____

5. *Watashi wa mainichi 7ji ni gakkoo o ikimasu.*
   わたしは　まいにち７じに　がっこうをいきます。

   _____

6. *Watashi no kaisha no mae e aisukuriimuya san ga arimasu.*
   わたしのかいしゃのまえへ　アイスクリームやさんがあります。

   _____

7. *Koko ni tabako o sutte mo ii desu ka?*
   ここに　たばこをすってもいいですか。

   _____

8. *Nihon no tomodachi ni hisashiburi ni tegami de kakimashita.*
   にほんのともだちに　ひさしぶりに　てがみでかきました。

   _____

9. *Watashi no apaato kara Rokkiisanmyaku o miemasu.*
   わたしのアパートから　ロッキーさんみゃくを　みえます。

   _____

LESSON 23

	年	月	日
	曜日		番
名前			

10. *Otooto wa mainichi inu to issho ni kooen e sanpo e ikimasu.*
おとうとは　まいにち　いぬといっしょに　こうえんへ　さんぽへいきます。

_____

11. *Tookyoo wa Nyuu Yooku yori zutto zutto hiroi na toshi desu.*
とうきょうは　ニューヨークより　ずっとずっと　ひろいなとしです。

_____

12. *Kore to onaji yoo ni hoohoo de kaite kudasai.*
これとおなじように　ほうほうで　かいてください。

_____

13. *Onaji koto o nankai mo kurikaeshinai de kudasai.*
おなじことを　なんかいも　くりかえしないでください。

_____

14. *Sukoshi karai da to omoimasu.*
すこしからいだ　とおもいます。

_____

15. *Nihonjin wa yoku hatarakimasu to omoimasu.*
にほんじんは　よくはたらきます　とおもいます。

_____

16. *Kono kiiroi no hana wa kaaneeshon desu ne.*
このきいろいのはなは　カーネーションですね。

_____

17. *Nihon ni tsukunara sugu denwa o shite ne.*
にほんにつくなら　すぐでんわをしてね。

_____

8. *Tenkiyohoo ni yoruto kyoo no gogo wa ame ga furisoo desu.*
てんきよほうによると　きょうのごごは　あめがふりそうです。

_____

LESSON 24

(A) This chart will test your knowledge of Japanese homonyms: words that have the same spelling and pronounciation but different meanings. Fill in the blanks of the chart with the Japanese homonym and its two different English meanings. The first one has been done for you.

	Nihongo	**English 1**	**English 2**
1	*hayai*	early	fast
2	*kiru*		
3		flower	
4	*yoku*		
5		visit	
6		frog	
7	*furu*		
8		paper	
9		bridge	
10	*uchi*		
11	*kakeru*		
12		affix/stick	
13	*yaku*		
14		meet	
15	*kanji*		
16		blow	
17	*hiku*		
18	*jishin*		
19	*okoru*		
20		buy	

90

	年	月	日
		曜日	番
名前			

B) Based on the English sentences, fill in the blanks with the correct Japanese translation using the passive tense.

1. *Sono repooto wa* _____ .

   そのレポートは _____ 。

   The report was written in Chinese.

2. *Watashi no* _____ .

   わたしの _____ 。

   My name was erased.

3. *Koora wa* _____ .

   コーラは _____ 。

   Cola is drunk everywhere in the world.

4. *Kare wa* _____ .

   これは _____ 。

   He was taught Japanese by his father.

5. *Metoroporitan myuujiamu no mon wa* _____ .

   メトロポリタンミュージアムのもんは _____ 。

   The (gate of the) Metropolitan Museum closes at 6pm.

6. *Amerika de mo nihonshoku no toki wa* _____ .

   アメリカでも　にほんしょくのときは _____ 。

   Chopsticks are used to eat Japanese food in America, too.

7. *Kono hon wa* _____ .

   このほんは _____ 。

   This book is well read in China.

8. *Kono osatsu* wa _____ .

   このおさつは _____ 。

   This bill is not being used any more.

9. *Ittoo shookin wa* _____ .

   いっとうしょうきんは _____ 。

   The first prize money was divided among three golf players.

年		月		日
	曜日			番
名前				

(C) Following are several notices or announcements written in English. Using --- *yoo desu*, translate each notice into Japanese and tell a friend what it says. Follow the example.

Example: "Please form line here."

   Koko ni narabu yoo desu.   ここに　ならぶようです。

1. "Do not enter."

   _____

2. "No turn on red."

   _____

3. "No food or beverages allowed."

   _____

4. "No pets allowed."

   _____

5. "Don't feed the animals."

   _____

6. "Beach closes after dark."

   _____

7. "Please use other door."

   _____

8. "Buy tickets here."

   _____

	年	月	日
		曜日	番
名前			

D) Fill in the blanks with a verb from the box below. Conjugate the verbs into the *-teru* ending, which is the shortened version of *-te iru*.

1. *Dare ka mukoo de* _____ *yo.*　だれかむこうで_____よ。

2. *Neko ga boku no okazu o* _____ *yo.*　ねこが　ぼくのおかずを_____よ。

3. *Mite, mite, Bobii ga isshookenmei ji o* _____.
   みて、みて、ボビーがいっしょうけんめい　じを_____。

4. *Terebi o* _____*kara benkyoo suru jikan ga nai no yo.*
   テレビを_____から　べんきょうするじかんがないのよ。

5. _____*ko o okosu na.*　_____こを　おこすな。

6. *Ima* _____*hon wa asu kaesu ne.*　いま_____ほんは　あすかえすね。

7. *Ima* _____*CD kiita?*　いま_____CD　きいた。

8. *Kochira ni mukatte* _____*hito wa nihongo no sensei desu.*
   こちらにむかって_____ひとは　にほんごのせんせいです。

9. *Asoko de* _____*ko wa kega o shita n ja nai?*
   あそこで_____こは　けがをしたんじゃない。

10. *Ima puuru de* _____*hitotachi ga Amerika no 400 meetoru riree chiimu da soo desu yo.*
    いまプールで_____ひとたちが　アメリカの４００メートルリレーチーム　だそうですよ。

---

aruku あるく, *kaku* かく, *kariru* かりる, *kasu* かす, *miru* みる, *naku* なく, *neru* ねる, *oyogu* およぐ, *taberu* たべる, *tatsu* たつ, *yobu* よぶ

年	月	日
	曜日	番
名前		

(E) Use the Internet or any other resource to find the answers to the following cultural questions

1. Judo is a traditional Japanese sport that is now internationally recognized. Judo is very complex because of the numerous skills and techniques that must be learned to master the sport Make a list in both Japanese and English of the different techniques (*waza*) used in judo.

2. Below is a diagram of a *dohyoo*, a sumo mound or ring. In Japanese, label the different parts of the *dohyoo*. Write the answers on the spaces provided.

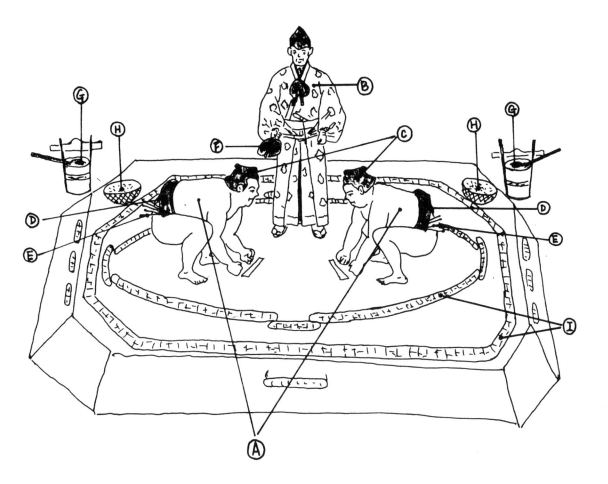

A _____ B _____

C _____ D _____

E _____ F _____

G _____ H _____

I _____

(A) Find and circle 12 words from Lesson 25 that are hidden in the chart below. They are written horizontally, vertically, diagonally, and backwards. There is no word list.

A	K	S	O	K	F	O	T	I	A
N	U	U	H	S	I	A	R	A	T
I	P	I	E	S	S	I	U	N	I
N	U	N	R	Y	K	F	I	E	H
U	I	O	U	E	U	U	B	R	S
K	E	M	M	S	K	T	I	U	A
A	R	I	U	O	Z	A	M	S	D
K	H	J	W	S	M	R	E	A	H
S	U	K	U	N	A	I	A	W	S
I	C	H	I	D	O	Y	T	G	A

	年	月	日
	曜日		番
名前			

B) Complete the following sentences with one of the two choices written below. Then use --- *kara* or --- *dakara* to explain your choice. Follow the example.

    (a) *to toku desu yo.* (positive, fortunate)   (b) *to son desu yo.* (negative, unfortunate)
      と　とくですよ。   と　そんですよ。

Example: *Gakkoo o yasumu* (b)   がっこうを　やすむ　（ b ）。
         Benkyoo ga okureru kara.   <u>べんきょうが　おくれるから。</u>

1. *Se ga takai* (　　　).   せがたかい　（　　　）。

    _____

2. *Omise de kuupon o tsukatte kaimono o suru* (　　　).
    おみせで　クーポンをつかって　かいものをする　（　　　）。

    _____

3. *Ji ga kirei da* (　　　).   じが　きれいだ　（　　　）。

    _____

4. *Gyanburu ga suki da* (　　　)   ギャンブルが　すきだ　（　　　）。

    _____

5. *Gaikokugo ga hanaseru* (　　　).   がいこくごが　はなせる。

    _____

6. *Ryoori ga kirai da* (　　　).   りょうりが　きらいだ　（　　　）。

    _____

7. *Kuchi ga karui* (　　　).   くちがかるい　（　　　）。

    _____

8. *Kao ga hiroi* (　　　).   かおがひろい　（　　　）。

    _____

LESSON 25

(C) Fill in the blanks of the following sentences with *tatta*, *mo*, or *shika*.

1. *Kinoo no miitingu ni kita hito wa _____ 3nin desu.*

    きのうのミーティングにきたひとは_____3にんです。

2. *Natsuyasumi made 1shuukan _____ arimasu.*

    なつやすみまで　1しゅうかん_____あります。

3. *Shingakki made 1shuukan _____ arimasen.*

    しんがっきまで　1しゅうかん_____ありません。

4. *Ninki chiimu datta node 1man nin _____ ooku okyakusan ga haitta.*

    にんきチームだったので　1まんにん_____おおく　おきゃくさんが　はいった。

5. *_____ 5nin ja shiai ga dekinai yo.*

    _____5にんじゃ　しあいができないよ。

6. *Kochira no okome wa 1000en _____ takai no ne.*

    こちらのおこめは　1000えん_____たかいのね。

7. *Kono kechappu to sore to 50sento _____ chigawanai yo.*

    このケチャップと　それと　50セント_____ちがわないよ。

8. *Kinoo _____ omiyage o kai ni iku jikan ga nakatta no?*

    きのう_____おみやげをかいにいくじかんが　なかったの。

9. *Shinsha o katte _____ mikka _____ notte inai noni moo koshoo shita n desu.*

    しんしゃをかって_____みっか_____のっていないのに　もう　こしょうしたんです。

10. *Onaji hon nanoni 100en _____ chigau no.*

    おなじほんなのに　100えん_____ちがうの。

年	月	日
	曜日	番
名前		

A) Complete the following sentences with words or phrases from Lesson 26.

1. _____ ga deta toki wa, byooin e iku hoo ga ii desu yo.

　_____ がでたときは、びょういんへいくほうが　いいですよ。

2. *Nihon ya Kanada de wa* _____ *o tsukai,* _____ *de wa kashi o tsukaimasu.*

　にほんやカナダでは_____をつかい、_____では　かしをつかいます。

3. A: *Hachigatsu Tookyoo de wa taitei* _____ *desu ka?*

　B: _____ *kashi 85do da to omoimasu.*

　A: はちがつ　とうきょうでは　たいてい_____ですか。

　B: _____かし８５ど　だとおもいます。

4. *Otoko no ko wa jitensha kara ochite,* _____.

　おとこのこは　じてんしゃからおちて、_____。

5. *Kenji kun, sooji shita* _____ *dakara, soto de asobinasai.*

　けんじくん、そうじした_____だから、そとであそびなさい。

6. *Hachijuuyon* _____ *juuni wa nana desu.*

　はちじゅうよん_____じゅうには　ななです。

7. *Senshuu Furorida shuu de wa* _____ *deshita. Taihen atsukatta wa.*

　せんしゅう　フロリダしゅうでは_____でした。たいへんあつかったわ。

8. A: *Kondo no doyoobi, horaa eiga o mi ni ikanai?*

　B: *Ano,* _____ *eiga wa chotto .....*

　A: こんどのどようび、ホラーえいがを　みにいかない。

　B: あの、_____えいがはちょっと. . .

9. _____ *shio to koshoo o kakete, sorekara 45fun yakimasu.*

　_____しおとこしょうを　かけて、それから　４５ふんやきます。

99

年	月	日
	曜日	番
名前		

(B) Change the given sentences from the third person to the point of view of the person stated b
using *-te kureru*. Follow the example.

Example: Third person → *Kinoo Yoshiko san wa Bobu san ni chuugakkoo jidai no arubamu*
misete agemashita.
きのう　よしこさんは　ボブさんに　ちゅうがっこうじだいの　アル
ムを　みせてあげました。

Bobu → <u>*Kinoo Yoshiko san ga chuugakkoo jidai no arubamu o miset*</u>
<u>*kuremashita.*</u>
<u>きのう　よしこさんが　ちゅうがっこうじだいの　アルバムを　みせ</u>
<u>くれました。</u>

1. Third person → *Tomu san wa tonari no kodomo ni Nihon no sumoo ni tsuite hanashi*
agemashita. トムさんは　となりのこどもに　にほんのすもう
ついて　はなしてあげました。

Kodomo → _____

2. Third person → *Hiroshi kun wa obaachan o kuruma de byooin made okutt*
agemashita. ひろしくんは　おばあちゃんを　くるまで　びょういんま
おくってあげました。

Obaachan → _____

3. Third person → *Piitaa san ga Keiko san no apaato sagashi o tetsudatte agemashit*
ピーターさんが　けいこさんのアパートさがしを　てつだってあげました。

Keiko → _____

4. Third person → *Risa san ga Ken chan ni eigo o oshiete agemashita.*
リサさんが　けんちゃんに　えいごを　おしえてあげました。

Ken no okaasan → _____

5. Third person → *Piitaa san wa Hiroshi kun ni Nomo no nyuusu o tsutaete agemashit*
ピーターさんは　ひろしくんに　のものニュースを　つたえてあげました。

Hiroshi no oniisan → _____

LESSON 26

(C) Complete each of the following sentences with a verb from the box below. Then conjugate the verb into the correct tense based on the context and form of the sentence. Various verb tenses are used in this exercise. Not all of the verbs in the box are used.

1. *Watashi no suki na kono hon wa Tomu Kuranshii ni yotte (   ) shoosetsu desu.*
   わたしのすきな　このほんは　トムクランシーによって　（　　　　　　　）しょうせつです。

2. *Motto ooki na koe de hanashite kudasai. Ongaku ga chotto urusai kara yoku (   ).*
   もっとおおきなこえで　はなしてください。おんがくが　ちょっとうるさいから　よく　（　　　　　）。

3. *Basu wa chotto osoi kara, Tookyoo made shinkansen ni (   ).*
   バスは　ちょっとおそいから、とうきょうまで　しんかんせんに　（　　　　　　　）。

4. *Imooto no tanjoobi wa raishuu no kayoobi dakara ima kara purezento o kai ni mooru ni (   ).*
   いもうとのたんじょうびは　らいしゅうのかようびだから　いまからプレゼントをかいに　モールに
   （　　　　　　　）。

5. *Warui seiseki o tottara, sensei to (   ) ii to omoimasu.*
   わるいせいせきをとったら、せんせいと　（　　　　　　）いいとおもいます。

6. *Atarashii no o konbiniensu sutoa de (   ).*
   あたらしいのを　コンビニエンスストアで　（　　　　　　）。

7. *Minasan, ato sukoshi ryoori ga (   ). Minna tabete kudasai.*
   みなさん、あとすこし　りょうりが　（　　　　　）。みんなたべてください。

8. *Kinoo kazoku to otera e itte, sosen no rei o (   ).*
   きのう　かぞくと　おてらへいって、そせんのれいを　（　　　　　　）。

9. *Kono nimotsu wa Furansu e (   ) no desu. Doo sureba ii desu ka?*
   このにもつは　フランスへ　（　　　　　　）のです。どうすればいいですか。

10. *Yuube koohii o nomisugita node, yoku (   ) deshita.*
    ゆうべ　コーヒーをのみすぎたので、よく　（　　　　　　）でした。

---

hanasu はなす, *iku* いく, *kaku* かく, *kau* かう, *kiku* きく, *kiru* きる, *kuru* くる, *nagusameru* なぐさめる, *nemuru* ねむる, *neru* ねる, *nokoru* のこる, *noru* のる, *okuru* おくる, *suru* する, *toru* とる,

LESSON 27

年	月	日
曜日		番
名前		

(A) Fill in the blank spaces of the following verb conjugation chart. The verbs are from Lessons 22, 23, 25, and 26 as well as from Volume One.

#	Dictionary Form	-ta Form	-teru (-te iru) ending	English: -ta Form
1		dashita		
2	hajimeru			
3				spoke, told
4	heru			
5	hiku			
6		itta		
7				called, locked
8				heard, listened, asked
9	kuru			
10	miru			
11				cried
12			okutteru	
13		otta		
14		shinda		
15			shitteru	
16	sumu			
17		shita		
18				continued
19	waru			
20				read

	年	月	日
	曜日		番
名前			

B) For each group of four words below, circle the one which does not belong with the others. Words are grouped based on their meanings. On the space provided, write the reason why the word does not belong to the group. You may answer in Japanese or English.

1. *waru*　わる,　*kakaru*　かかる,　*hiku*　ひく,　*kakeru*　かける

　　_____

2. *inchi*　インチ,　*fiito*　フィート,　*kiroguramu*　キログラム,　*mairu*　マイル

　　_____

3. *shio*　しお,　*satoo*　さとう,　*shooyu*　しょうゆ,　*yaku*　やく

　　_____

4. *ame*　あめ,　*jishin*　じしん,　*taifuu*　たいふう,　*ooyuki*　おおゆき

　　_____

5. *shiidii pureeya*　ＣＤプレーヤー,　*bideokamera*　ビデオカメラ,　*rajikase*　ラジカセ
　　uookuman　ウォークマン

　　_____

6. *chirashizushi*　ちらしずし,　*osake*　おさけ,　*okonomiyaki*　おこのみやき,　*misoshiru*　みそしる

　　_____

7. *tanka*　たんか,　*kossetsu*　こっせつ,　*nenza*　ねんざ,　*kega*　けが

　　_____

8. *shinpai*　しんぱい,　*koofun*　こうふん,　*utsukushii*　うつくしい,　*kanashii*　かなしい

　　_____

9. *kibun ga warui*　きぶんがわるい,　*netsu*　ねつ,　*daijoobu*　だいじょうぶ,
　　nodo ga itai　のどがいたい

　　_____

0. *yomu*　よむ,　*taberu*　たべる,　*tsukuru*　つくる,　*yaku*　やく

　　_____

1. *Nihon*　にほん,　*Kankoku*　かんこく,　*Igirisu*　イギリス,　*Chuugoku*　ちゅうごく

　　_____

2. *yukata*　ゆかた,　*oshoogatsu*　おしょうがつ,　*bon'odori*　ぼんおどり,　*yatai*　やたい

103

年	月	日
曜日		番
名前		

(C) Using *to omou*, answer the following questions with the given words. Answer questions 6 and 7 with your own ideas. Follow the example.

Example: *Kono mondai ni tsuite doo omoimasu ka?* → *Taihen muzukashii*
このもんだいについて　どうおもいますか。　→　たいへんむずかしい
Taihen muzukashii mondai da to omoimasu.
たいへんむずかしいもんだいだ　とおもいます。

1. *Gaikoku ryokoo ni tsuite doo omoimasu ka?* → *Taihen benkyoo ni narimasu*
がいこくりょこうについて　どうおもいますか。→　たいへんべんきょうになります

_____

2. *Kotoshi no puroyakyuu wa doo naru to omoimasu ka?* → *Hiroshima ga yuushoo shimasu*
ことしのプロやきゅうは　どうなるとおもいますか。→　ひろしまが　ゆうしょうします

_____

3. *Nijuunen go no komyunikeeshon wa doo naru to omoimasu ka?* → *Terebidenwa de hanasemas*
にじゅうねんごの　コミュニケーションは　どうなるとおもいますか。→　テレビでんわで　はなせま

_____

4. *Denkijidoosha ni tsuite doo omoimasu ka?* → *Ichido notte mitai desu*
でんきじどうしゃについて　どうおもいますか。→　いちど　のってみたいです

_____

5. *Doo ka shimashita ka?* → *Koko ni megane o wasurete ikimashita*
どうかしましたか。→　ここに　めがねを　わすれていきました。

_____

6. *Anata wa nihongo no benkyoo ni tsuite doo omotte imasu ka?*
あなたは　にほんごのべんきょうについて　どうおもっていますか。

_____

7. *Anata wa shoorai nani ni naritai to omotte imasu ka?*
あなたは　しょうらい　なにになりたいとおもっていますか。

_____

年	月	日
曜日		番
名前		

D) Following are three "word problems" which will give you the opportunity to practice arithmetic in Japanese. Read each one and answer the questions.

1. *Futatsu no suuji A to B o tasu to 30 ni narimasu. A kara B o hiku to 2 ni narimasu. A to B wa sorezore ikutsu desu ka?*
   ふたつのすうじ　AとBをたすと　３０になります。AからBをひくと　２になります。AとBは
   それぞれ　いくつですか。
   A = _____   B = _____

2. *280en ni 12 o kakete dete kita suuji o 30 de waru to kotae wa ikutsu ni narimasu ka?*
   ２８０えんに　１２をかけて　でてきたすうじを　３０でわると　こたえはいくつになりますか。
   Answer = _____

3. *Piitaa san to Nanshii san wa Taroo kun to issho ni Nihon resutoran de shokuji o suru koto ni shimashita. Kono resutoran ni wa Nihon no ryoori ga nan demo arimashita. Piitaa san ga chuumon shita oyakodonburi to misoshiru wa sorezore 890en to 180en deshita. Nanshii san wa nigirizushi to sarada o tanomimashita. Sorezore 1200en to 360en deshita. Taroo kun wa nabeyakiudon to inarizushi o tabemashita. Nedan wa sorezore 850en to 600en deshita. Shokuji no ato 3nin tomo dezaato o taberu koto ni shimashita. Piitaa san wa 350en no maccha aisukuriimu, Nanshii san wa 400en no meron, soshite Taroo kun wa 450en no shaabetto ni shimashita. Sorezore 3nin ga tabeta shokuji to sono nedan o hyoo (chart) ni kaite keisan shite kudasai.*
   ピーターさんと　ナンシーさんは　たろうくんといっしょに　にほんレストランで　しょくじをす
   ることにしました。このレストランには　にほんのりょうりが　なんでもありました。ピーターさ
   んが　ちゅうもんした　おやこどんぶりとみそしるは　それぞれ８９０えんと１８０えんでした。
   ナンシーさんは　にぎりずしとサラダを　たのみました。それぞれ１２００えんと３６０えんでし
   た。たろうくんは　なべやきうどんといなりずしを　たべました。ねだんはそれぞれ８５０えんと
   ６００えんでした。しょくじのあと　３にんとも　デザートをたべることにしました。ピーターさ
   んは　３５０えんのまっちゃアイスクリーム、ナンシーさんは　４００えんのメロン、そして　た
   ろうくんは　４５０えんのシャーベットにしました。それぞれ３にんがたべたしょくじと　そのね
   だんを　ひょうにかいて　けいさんしてください。

	Piitaa	*Nanshii*	*Taroo*
chuumon shita tabemono			
nedan no gookei (total price)			

105

LESSON 28

(A) Create your own original sentences using both of the given words. Verbs may be used in any tense, and the given words may be used in any order. Try to make sentences that are different from the Sample Conversation.

1. *kangaekata* かんがえかた, *kuni* くに _____

_____

2. *chigau* ちがう, *zenbu* ぜんぶ _____

_____

3. *reisenjidai* れいせんじだい, *chikyuu* ちきゅう _____

_____

4. *iroiro na* いろいろな, *kokusaimondai* こくさいもんだい _____

_____

5. *owaru* おわる, *sanka suru* さんかする _____

_____

6. *orinpikku* オリンピック, *kyooryoku* きょうりょく _____

_____

7. *nihonryokoo* にほんりょこう, *yasumi* やすみ _____

_____

B) Ask someone if they could do something for you based on each of the following situations. Use the expression --- *o -te kurenai?* in writing each question.

Example: Both of your hands are full and you cannot open the door. Ask your friend ...
   Doa o akete kurenai?   ドアをあけてくれない。

1. You need a ride home after a party. A friend who lives near you is driving home. Ask him/her ...

   _____

2. While walking home from school, you want to write something down but can't hold your bag and the notebook at the same time. Ask your friend ...

   _____

3. You are eating dinner at home and want some soy sauce, but it's at the other end of the table. Ask someone ...

   _____

4. You want one of your classmates to write his/her address on a piece of paper. Ask him/her ...

   _____

5. It is late, but your roommate wants to talk. You wish he/she would go to sleep. Ask him/her ...

   _____

6. Your teacher needs someone to erase the blackboard. He/She asks a student ...

   _____

7. Your mother needs the white box on the shelf, but she cannot reach it. She asks you ...

   _____

	年	月	日
	曜日		番
名前			

(C) Following the example, tell your friends not to do the following actions or things. Make sure you conjugate the verbs correctly. Write the new sentence, in either *roomaji* or *hiragana*, on the top line. Then tranlate the new sentence into English and write it on the bottom line.

Example: *Shinpai suru* . → <u>*Shinpai shinai de kudasai*</u>. → <u>Please don't worry</u>.
しんぱいする。 → しんぱいしないでください。

1. *Hajimeru.* → <u>Mada</u> _____
   はじめる _____

2. *Kenka suru.* → _____
   けんかする _____

3. *Jitto mitsumeru* (stare). → _____
   じっとみつめる _____

4. *Hashi o ochawan ni tateru.* → _____
   はしを　おちゃわんにたてる。 _____

5. *Kutsu o haite agaru.* → _____
   くつをはいて　あがる _____

6. *Jugyoo chuu ni nemuru.* → _____
   じゅぎょうちゅうに　ねむる _____

7. *Shukudai o wasureru.* → _____
   しゅくだいを　わすれる _____

8. *Warui koto o suru.* → _____
   わるいことを　する _____

9. *Shitsurei na koto o iu.* → _____
   しつれいなことを　いう _____

10. *Ooki na koe de hanasu.* → _____
    おおきなこえで　はなす _____

11. *Densha no nake de mono o taberu.* → _____
    でんしゃのなかで　ものをたべる _____

12. *Heya no naka de booshi o kaburu* → _____
    へやのなかで　ぼうしをかぶる _____

LESSON 29

年	月	日
曜日		番
名前		

A) Complete the following crossword puzzle. Words and clues are taken mostly from Lessons 28 and 29 as well as from previous lessons. All answers are in Japanese. For English clues in quotations, the answer is the Japanese translation.

CROSS

1. _____ wa tokidoki sensoo (war) ni naru.
7. 1996 nen no natsu _____ wa Atoranta de arimashita.
8. Nihonjin wa _____ toki, taitei hashi o tsukaimasu.
9. Kaigai _____ suru tame, pasupooto ga hitsuyoo desu.
12. Chotto _____ ne ..... Piitaa, odenwa desu.
13. Watashi no kuruma ni wa kootsuu anzen (safe driving) no _____ ga arimasu.
15. 8ji ni tomodachi ni _____ no? Moo 9ji desu yo.
17. Nihon de wa nansai kara kuruma o _____ suru koto ga dekimasu ka?
20. Gakkoo de, sakkaa o shite nenza shita toki, _____ e ikimashita.
21. Ryokoo ni wa _____ ii kisetsu desu.

DOWN

1. Sekaijuu no kuni ga _____ sureba, sekai wa anzen ni naru kamo shirenai.
2. Watashi no apaato wa 12 _____ ni arimasu.
3. Kita Nihon ni aru tokai.
4. Kitte o hatte, tegami o _____.
5. Nara ni aru kankoo supotto.
6. Futari no shiawase o _____.
10. Opposite of "hajimatta."
11. Mukashi no hito wa _____ wa taira (flat) da to omotte ita.
14. Taipu wa _____ arimasu. Hitotsu o erande kudasai.
15. Paatii de kiru atarashii yoofuku o _____.
18. _____ ga itai. Kaze o hiita ka na.
19. Ima made ni ryokoo shita _____ wa doko desu ka?

109

LESSON 29

(B) In this exercise you will write your own sentences using *Issho ni --- -mashoo*. In your sentence include the word that has been given for each problem. Follow the example.

Example: *suugaku to eigo*   すうがくと　えいご
    Issho ni suugaku to eigo o benkyoo shimashoo.
    いっしょに　すうがくとえいごを　べんきょうしましょう。

1. *kafeteria*   カフェテリア

    _____

2. *gakkoo*   がっこう

    _____

3 *terebi no ninki bangumi*   テレビの　にんきばんぐみ

    _____

4. *tegami to shashin*   てがみとしゃしん

    _____

5. *jinja*   じんじゃ

    _____

6. *atarashii CD*   あたらしいCD

    _____

7. *takushii*   タクシー

    _____

8. *mizu to kusuri*   みずとくすり

    _____

	年 月	日
	曜日	番
名前		

C) In each of the following conversations, B's part has been given in response to what A has asked. From the list in the box below, choose the correct question for A and write the letter on the line.

1. A: _____
   B: *Choodo ii yu desu.*
   ちょうどいい　ゆです。

2. A: _____
   B: *Sukoshi karai to omoimasu.*
   すこしからい　とおもいます。

3. A: _____
   B: *Choodo ii nagasa da to omoimasu.*
   ちょうどいい　ながさだとおもいます。

4. A: _____
   B: *Sukoshi hosoi yoo desu.*
   すこしほそい　ようです。

5. A: _____
   B: *Kanari kurai to omoimasu.*
   かなりくらい　とおもいます。

6. A: _____
   B: *Daibun chiisai yoo desu.*
   だいぶんちいさい　ようです。

7. A: _____
   B: *Kanari osoi desu yo.*
   かなりおそいですよ。

8. A: _____
   B: *Sukoshi yawarakai desu.*
   すこしやわらかいです。

---

a. *Akarusa wa doo desu ka?*
あかるさは　どうですか。

b. *Futosa wa doo desu ka?*
ふとさは　どうですか。

c. *Hayasa wa doo desu ka?*
はやさは　どうですか。

d. *Katasa wa doo desu ka?*
かたさは　どうですか。

e. *Nagasa wa doo desu ka?*
ながさは　どうですか。

f. *Oaji wa doo desu ka?*
おあじは　どうですか。

g. *Ookisa wa doo desu ka?*
おおきさは　どうですか。

h. *Yukagen wa doo desu ka?*
ゆかげんは　どうですか。

111

LESSON 30

(A) Translate the following English words into Japanese and the Japanese words into English. Th words are from various lessons in this volume.

	English	Nihongo
1		*shimekiri*
2		*kakunin suru*
3		*jidoo*
4		*shiai*
5		*nengajoo*
6		*chikyuu*
7		*shuukyoo*
8		*nioi*
9		*kamaimasen*
10		*tsuzukeru*
11	high fever	
12	to remember	
13	Buddhism	
14	weather forecast	
15	remain	
16	electronics	
17	to die	
18	freely	
19	to participate	
20	natural	

LESSON 30

年	月	日
	曜日	番
名前		

B) The three words in each group all start with the same phonetic sound of the Japanese language. Fill in each square with one sound to complete the three words. Then translate each word into English. Most of the words are from Volume Two; some are from Volume One. Follow the example.

Example: | to |
- kai ⟷ big city
- mato ⟷ tomato
- kei ⟷ watch

1. ☐
- ru ⟷ _____
- shi ⟷ _____
- ko ⟷ _____

2. ☐
- ma ⟷ _____
- ku ⟷ _____
- mi ⟷ _____

3. ☐
- ka ⟷ _____
- gau ⟷ _____
- kai ⟷ _____

4. ☐
- sho ⟷ _____
- bun ⟷ _____
- shin ⟷ _____

5. ☐
- wai ⟷ _____
- ze ⟷ _____
- rui ⟷ _____

6. ☐
- mui ⟷ _____
- tsu ⟷ _____
- nza ⟷ _____

7. ☐
- tae ⟷ _____
- me ⟷ _____
- wai ⟷ _____

8. ☐
- ru ⟷ _____
- nka ⟷ _____
- kura ⟷ _____

9. ☐
- goto ⟷ _____
- zen ⟷ _____
- ken ⟷ _____

10. ☐
- kau ⟷ _____
- gi ⟷ _____
- yoi ⟷ _____

113

年	月	日
	曜日	番
名前		

(C) Each of the following pair of words shares one phonetic sound of the Japanese language. Fill in the squares with the correct sound to make two Japanese words. Then translate the two words into English, listing the horizontal word first. Follow the example.

Example: *a* □ *ma*   <u>head</u>

      fu (top) *ri* (bottom)   <u>two people</u>

1. *ka* □ *ii*   _____
    o (top) *ru* (bottom)   _____

2. *ha* □ *su*   _____
    to (top) *ri* (bottom)   _____

3. *ko* □ *ru*   _____
    na (top) *e* (bottom)   _____

4. *chi* □ *u*   _____
    hi (top) *shi* (bottom)   _____

5. *chi* □ *n*   _____
    ni (top) *u* (bottom)   _____

6. *o* □ *ru*   _____
    ko (top) *mo* (bottom)   _____

7. *de* □ *ru*   _____
    re (top) *shi* (bottom)   _____

8. *sa* □ *mi*   _____
    a (top) *ta* (bottom)   _____

9. *tsu* □ *ri*   _____
    o (top) *u* (bottom)   _____

10. *ka* □ *ru*   _____
    se (top) *i* (bottom)   _____

D) The following is a telephone conversation between two friends, Nancy and Akemi. They are talking about Nancy's upcoming trip to Japan. Based on the context of the conversation, fill in the blanks with the letter of the most appropriate sentence from those listed below.

Nancy: *Moshi moshi, watashi Nanshii desu.* 1._____   もしもし、わたしナンシーです。1._____

Akemi: *A! Nanshii. Watashi Akemi. Nihonryokoo daibu chikazuite kita wa ne.* 2._____
あ！ナンシー。わたしあけみ。にほんりょこう　だいぶちかづいてきたわね。2._____

Nancy: *Un. Jitsu wa sono koto nan dakedo, 3gatsu wa futsuu* 3._____
うん。じつは　そのことなんだけど、3がつはふつう3._____

Akemi: *Soo ne, Tookyoo no 3gatsu wa daibu atatakaku natte iru kara,* 4._____
そうね、とうきょうの3がつは　だいぶあたたかくなっているから、4._____

Nancy: *Jaa, hansode demo ii kashira.* 5._____   じゃあ、はんそででもいいかしら。5._____

Akemi: *Hansode? Sore wa chotto hayasugiru to omou wa. Datte sesshi de daitai 15do gurai yo.*
はんそで？それはちょっとはやすぎる　とおもうわ。だってせっしで　だいたい１５どぐらいよ。

Nancy: *15do gurai tte,* 6._____   １５どぐらいって、6._____

Akemi: *60do gurai ne. Demo asa to yoru wa mada daibun samui wa yo.*
６０どぐらいね。でも　あさとよるは　まだだいぶんさむいわよ。

Nancy: *Jaa nagasode no jaketto mo motte itta hoo ga* 7._____
じゃあ　ながそでのジャケットも　もっていったほうが7._____

Akemi: *Soo shita hoo ga ii wa yo.*　そうしたほうがいいわよ。

Nancy: *Arigatoo. Sorekara hikooki no yoyaku mo shita kara* 8._____ *oku wa ne.*
ありがとう。それから　ひこうきのよやくもしたから8._____　おくわね。

Akemi: *Chotto matte ne.* 9._____ *Ii wa yo.*　ちょっとまってね。9._____　いいわよ。

Nancy: *Nihon toochaku wa 3gatsu 15nichi. Hikooki wa Yuunaiteddo no 801bin, soshite Narita* 10._____ *gogo 3ji han yo.*
にほんとうちゃくは　3がつ１５にち。ひこうきは　ユーナイテッドの８０１びん、そして　なりた10._____　ごご3じはんよ。

Akemi: *Moo ichido* 11._____   もういちど 11._____

Nancy: *801bin yo.*　８０１びんよ。

Akemi: *Wakatta wa. Kuukoo made* 12._____　わかったわ。くうこうまで12._____

Nancy: *Arigatoo. Sore jaa mata renraku suru wa.*　ありがとう。それじゃあまたれんらくするわ。

a. *furaito bangoo o itte*　　フライトばんごうを　いって

b. *Dekiru dake nimotsu o herashitai no.*　　できるだけ　にもつを　へらしたいの。

c. *mukae ni iku kara ne.*　　むかえにいくからね。

d. *Akemi san onegai shimasu.*　　あけみさん　おねがいします。

e. *Memo no yooi o suru kara.*　　メモのよういをするから。

f. *Ryokoo no junbi susunderu?*　　りょこうのじゅんび　すすんでる。

g. *yosasoo ne.*　　よさそうね。

h. *toochaku wa*　　とうちゃくは

i. *kooto wa iranai to omou wa.*　　コートはいらない　とおもうわ。

j. *kashi de ieba dono gurai kashira?*　　かしでいえば　どのぐらいかしら。

k. *donna fuku o kite iru?*　　どんなふくを　きている。

l. *Nihon toochaku no jikan o itte*　　にほんとうちゃくのじかんを　いって。

VOCABULARY LIST

SC = Sample Conversation
APE = Activity, Practice, & Exercise

(A)

abekobe	10	SC	reversed, opposite
achira	20	APE	over there
aete [*au*]	13	APE	meet, met
aida	1	APE	between, during
aisu tii	19	APE	iced tea
aite	20	APE	companion
aite iru [*aku*]	17	APE	be open
Ajia	19	SC	Asia
akemashite	16	SC	[literally] open
akeru	8	APE	to open
akusesarii	7	APE	accessories
ame	10	SC	rain
amimono	2	APE	knitting
amutorakku	4	SC	Amtrak
Arabu	28	APE	Arabian countries
arau	22	APE	to wash
asobi ni iku [*asobu*]	7	APE	go to play
atari	11	APE	right, correct
ate	2	SC	addressed to
atto iu ma	13	SC	in an instant

(B)

bakari	26	SC	just
bangohan	7	APE	dinner, supper
barentaindee	20	SC	Valentine's Day
basho	17	SC	place
benkyoo jikan	25	SC	study hour
benkyoo suru	2	APE	to study
Berugii	28	APE	Belgium
Betonamu	28	APE	Vietnam
bideokamera	14	APE	camcorder
biiru	20	APE	beer
binboo	5	APE	poor
bon'odori	4	SC	Bon Festival dance
boonenkai	4	APE	year-ending party
booru	25	APE	ball
buchoo	22	APE	director, department head
bukkyoo	19	SC	Buddhism
bunka	10	APE	culture

117

bunkasai	4	APE	cultural festival
burausu	14	APE	blouse
Burugaria	28	APE	Bulgaria
Busshu	28	APE	George Bush
butsukaru	26	APE	to hit, to strike
byooki	11	APE	sick

(C)

chansu	25	APE	chance
Chekosurobakia	28	APE	Czechoslovakia
chian	5	SC	public peace and order
chigau	28	SC	different
chiikifunsoo	28	SC	regional conflict/dispute
chika	25	APE	basement
chikai	8	SC	close
chikaku [*chikai*]	7	SC	near, close to
chikoku	19	APE	late
chikyuu	28	SC	a globe, Earth
chirashizushi	4	APE	a type of sushi
choko	20	SC	chocolate
choochoo	22	APE	butterfly
choodo	29	SC	just, perfect
Choosen	28	APE	Korea, Korean
chooshi	22	SC	condition
chotto	4	APE	a little
chuu	29	APE	be in the middle of
Chuugoku	19	SC	China
chuugokuryoori	19	SC	Chinese food
chuurippu	19	APE	tulip
chuusha	20	APE	shot, injection
chuushoku	22	APE	lunch

(D)

daibutsu	8	SC	Great Buddha
daijishin	25	APE	big earthquake
daisuki	11	SC	like very much
daitai	11	APE	about
daitokai	10	SC	big city, metropolis
dame	8	APE	not good, no use
dashimashita, dashita [*dasu*]	25	SC	submitted
dasu	25	APE	to send
datte	2	APE	they say, I hear

— de	26	SC	by ...., due to
dekakenakereba narimasen	11	APE	has/have to go out
dekita [*dekiru*]	8	SC	built
denkiseihin	14	SC	electrical appliances
densha	11	APE	train
denwa o kakeru	7	APE	to make a telephone call
depaato	19	APE	department store
dezaato	16	APE	dessert
do	10	APE	degree [temperature]
dochira	17	APE	which
Doitsu	5	APE	Germany
dono/dore kurai	8	APE	how much/many
doobutsuen	20	APE	zoo
doofuu shimasu	1	SC	enclose
doopingu	28	APE	drugs, doping
dooshite	11	APE	why
Doo suru?	2	APE	What shall/should we do?

(E)

ebi	19	APE	shrimp
eeto ...	19	SC	well ....
ehagaki	2	SC	[picture] postcard
eiga	2	APE	movie
enryo naku	17	SC	without reserve, hesitation
erabu	7	APE	to choose

(F)

fasshon	14	APE	fashion
fiito	26	APE	feet
Foodo	23	APE	Ford
Fujisan	4	APE	Mt. Fuji
fuku	16	APE	clothes
furafura	5	APE	be dizzy
furansugo o toru	7	APE	to take French [language]
furui	8	SC	old
Furushichofu	28	APE	Khrushchev
fushigi	17	SC	strange, mysterious
futari	25	SC	two people
futotta [*futoru*]	11	SC	gained weight
futte imasu [*furu*]	10	SC	is raining
fuukei	17	SC	scene
fuyu	5	APE	winter
fuyuyasumi	4	APE	winter vacation

(G)

gaikokujin	14	SC	foreigner
gaikokuryokoo	14	APE	travel abroad
ganbaru	1	APE	to persist in
.....gawa	4	APE	..... River
geki	17	APE	a play
gifuto	25	APE	gift
giri	20	SC	[social] duty, obligation
Girisha	19	APE	Greece
go	23	SC	after
gogo	10	SC	p.m.
Gomen ne.	2	APE	I'm sorry.
gomi	16	APE	trash, dirt
Gorubachofu	28	APE	Mikhail Gorbachev
gorufu	22	APE	golf
gozen	10	SC	a.m.
gurai/kurai	8	SC	about
guramu	26	APE	gram
gyuunyuu	19	APE	milk

(H)

hade	2	SC	showy, flamboyant, gaudy, laud
hairu	11	APE	to enter
haitte iru [*hairu*]	25	APE	be in, be contained
hajimete	5	SC	first time
hajimete kiita [*kiku*]	2	APE	never heard of that before
hakiyasui	23	APE	comfortable, easy to wear
hakken suru	8	APE	to discover
hako	16	APE	box
haku	11	APE	to wear
hakukbutsukan	17	APE	museum
hanashita [*hanasu*]	20	SC	talked, spoke
hanashite [*hanasu*]	10	SC	speak
hanbun	13	SC	half
Hangarii	28	APE	Hungary
hannin	13	APE	criminal
ha o migaku	10	APE	to brush one's teeth
hare	10	SC	clear, fine [weather]
hareru	14	APE	become clear [weather]
haru	25	APE	to put on, to stick
haruyasumi	4	APE	spring vacation
hashi	19	SC	chopsticks

hasseki	8	SC	the 8th century
hayai	4	SC	fast
hayaku [*hayai*]	7	APE	quickly, in a hurry
hazure	11	APE	wrong
hen	16	APE	strange
heru	25	SC	to reduce, become less
heta	16	APE	poor, be bad at
heya	7	APE	room
hidari no	17	SC	on the left
higashi	19	SC	east
Higashi Doitsu	28	APE	East Germany
hiite [*hiku*]	26	SC	minus, subtract, from
hikooki	5	SC	airplane
hipparidako	5	APE	be in great demand
hiru	10	SC	afternoon, daytime
hirugohan	2	APE	lunch
hiruyasumi	7	APE	lunch break, recess
hitori	4	APE	one person
hitori de	5	APE	alone
hitotsu zutsu	17	APE	one of each
Ho Chi-min	28	APE	Ho Chi Minh
hohoemu	22	APE	to smile
hoka de wa	8	SC	elsewhere, other places
hoka ni	19	SC	anything else
hokenshitsu	29	APE	health room
hone	23	SC	bone
Honkon	19	SC	Hong Kong
Hontoo da.	22	APE	It's true.
hontoo ni	13	APE	really
hontoo wa	2	SC	in fact, actually, really
hon'yaku	16	APE	translation
hookai suru	28	APE	to collapse
hoshii	14	SC	want
hoshiku natta [*hoshii*]	14	SC	wanted, has wanted
hotokesama	8	SC	Buddha
hyakudo	26	SC	100 degrees

(I)

ichiban	8	SC	the best, most, first
ichiban ii	14	APE	the best
ichido	25	SC	once, one time
ichinen	17	SC	a year, one year

ichinichi ni	29	APE	a day
igan	20	APE	stomach cancer
igo	2	APE	go [a game]
ieba [*iu*]	11	SC	be said
Igirisu	4	APE	England
ii yo	2	APE	O.K.
ijoo	25	APE	over, more than
ikaiyoo	20	APE	stomach ulcer
ikanai [*iku*]	8	SC	Aren't you...?
ikanai [*iku*]	23	SC	How about going to ...?
			Would you like to go to ...?
ikemasu [*iku*]	17	SC	can go
ikimasen [*iku*]	8	SC	Aren't you ...?
ikimashita [*iku*]	4	SC	went
iku	2	APE	to go
imi	5	SC	meaning, sense
imushitsu	23	SC	health room
inchi	26	APE	inch
inorimasu [*inoru*]	17	SC	pray
inoru	17	APE	to pray
ippai	5	APE	many, full
Irasshaimase.	19	APE	Please come in./May I help you?
— *irasshaimasu ka?*	29	APE	Is .... there?
ireru	8	APE	to put something in
iro	11	APE	color
iroiro na	28	SC	various
issei	25	SC	at the same time
issho ni	29	SC	together
isshookenmei	17	APE	with all one's might
itai	23	SC	hurt, be painful
Itaria	28	APE	Italy
itariaryoori	19	APE	Italian food
Itsumo osewa ni natte imasu.	5	APE	Thank you for taking care of me.
itta [*iku*]	1	SC	went, was in
itte [*iku*]	5	SC	go
itte kimashita [*iku, kuru*]	4	SC	have been to, went to
Ittekimasu.	5	APE	I'm off., I'll be back
Itterashai.	5	APE	[literally] Go and come back.
iu/yuu	16	SC	to say, to mean
iwarete [*iu*]	2	SC	to be told
iya	11	APE	unpleasant, disgusting
iyaringu	14	APE	earring

(J)

ja nakatta	5	APE	not, was not
jettokoosutaa	2	APE	roller coaster
ji	16	APE	characters, letters
jibun	2	SC	oneself
jibun no	13	APE	one's own
jidoo	11	SC	automatic
jidoosha	19	SC	automobile
jiinzu	11	APE	jeans
jiko	5	APE	accident
jikokuhyoo	17	APE	schedule [bus, train]
jinja	17	SC	shrine
jinkoo	5	APE	population
jisaboke	1	SC	jet lag
jishin	13	APE	earthquake
jishin	22	SC	confidence
jiyuu	8	SC	liberty, freedom
jiyuu ni	17	SC	freely
jiyuu no megami	8	SC	Statue of Liberty
Jonson	28	APE	Lyndon B. Johnson
joobu na	26	APE	healthy, well, strong
joodan	2	SC	joke, be kidding, tease
jookyuusei	19	APE	upperclassman
joozu ni nattara [*naru*]	19	APE	if ... become good at ...
jugyoo	4	SC	class
junban ni	17	APE	in turns
12gatsu tooka	4	APE	December 10th
juunijikan	5	SC	twelve hours
juunishi	16	SC	twelve animals of the Chinese twelve-year cycle

(K)

kabe	8	APE	wall
kaeru	11	SC	to go home
kaesu	16	APE	to return
kaette kita [*kaeru, kuru*]	5	APE	came back
kafeteria	2	APE	cafeteria
kagi o kakeru	7	APE	to lock
kaimasen [*kau*]	13	SC	does/did not buy
kaimono	14	SC	shopping
kaisan shokuhin	10	APE	seafood
kaitai [*kau*]	14	SC	want to buy

kakanakereba [*kaku*]	7	APE	has/have to write
kakaru	5	APE	to take [period of time]
kakete [*kakeru*]	26	SC	multiply, times
kakimasu [*kaku*]	1	SC	write, will write
kakkoii	4	APE	cool [style, personality]
kaku	2	APE	to write
kakunin shimasu	25	SC	confirm
kakunin shitai	17	SC	want to confirm
kamaimasen	17	SC	O.K., no problem
kameraya	7	SC	camera shop
kamo	22	SC	may, might
kamo shirenai	5	APE	maybe, may, might
kamu	22	APE	to chew
kanarazu	14	APE	certainly, surely
kanashisoo [*kanashii*]	22	APE	look sad
Kanbojia	28	APE	Cambodia
kangaekata [*kangaeru*]	28	SC	way of thinking
Kankoku	19	SC	Korea
kankokusei	19	SC	made in Korea
kankyookyaku	1	APE	tourist
kanojo	20	APE	girlfriend, she
kantan	16	SC	simple, in short
karada	26	APE	body
karakara	5	APE	be very thirsty
kara...made	5	APE	from ... to ....
kareshi	20	APE	boyfriend, he
kare tte	22	SC	he is
karichatte [*kariru*]	20	APE	borrow
kariru	8	APE	to borrow
karui	14	APE	light [weight]
kashi	26	SC	Fahrenheit
kashite [*kasu*]	16	SC	lend
kashite kureru [*kasu*]	26	APE	let one borrow
kashu	5	APE	singer
Kasutoro	28	APE	Fidel Castro
kateika	19	APE	home economics
katta [*kau*]	13	SC	bought
katte kita [*kau, kuru*]	2	SC	bought
kaubooi	19	APE	cowboy
kawai	7	APE	cute, pretty
kawaisoo	23	APE	feel sorry for [someone]
kaze o hiku	5	APE	to catch a cold

124

kazu	20	SC	number
keeki	25	APE	cake
kega	23	SC	injury
keisan shite	26	SC	calculate
Kenedii	28	APE	John F. Kennedy
kenka suru	14	APE	to fight
kenkoo	26	APE	health
kenkooshindan	25	SC	medical/physical examination, health check
kesu	25	APE	to turn off
kibishii	19	APE	strict
kibun ga warui	29	APE	feel sick
kikitai [*kiku*]	4	SC	would like to hear
kimashita [*kiru*]	4	SC	wore, put on
kimatsushiken	4	APE	term examination
kimi	29	SC	you
kinchoo suru	5	APE	be strained, stressed, nervous
kin'enseki	17	APE	no smoking seat
kinenshashin	11	SC	a souvenir photo
Kingashinnen.	16	SC	Happy New Year.
kingyo	7	SC	goldfish
ki ni itte	2	SC	be a favorite with, favor
kion	10	APE	temperature
ki o tsukeru	5	SC	be careful, to pay attention
Ki o tsukete.	5	SC	Take care., Pay attention
kippu	25	APE	ticket
kirei na ji de kaku	14	APE	write neat characters, write neatly
kiroguramu	26	APE	kilogram
kiromeetoru	26	APE	kilometer
kisetsuhazure	2	SC	out of season
kita [*kiru*]	7	SC	wore, wearing
Kita Amerika	28	APE	North America
kite [*kuru*]	13	SC	could come/came
kiteru [*kuru*]	14	SC	come, has come
kitsuenseki	17	APE	smoking seat
kochira	17	APE	this way
koibito	13	APE	lover
koinobori	2	SC	a carp streamer
Koka Koora	19	APE	Coca Cola
kokusaimondai	28	SC	international problems/issues
komaru	16	APE	be troubled, be in trouble
kome	19	SC	rice [uncooked]

konbiniensu sutoa	5	APE	convenience store
kondo	13	SC	this time
kondo no	2	APE	next
kono aida	14	APE	the other day
konogoro	19	APE	these days, recently
konpyuuta ruumu	19	APE	computer room
kontakuto renzu	16	APE	contact lens
koochoo sensei	17	APE	principal
koofun	5	SC	exciting, be excited
kookan shiyoo	2	SC	let's trade, let's exchange
kookan suru	20	APE	to exchange
kookuubin	17	APE	air mail
kookuugaisha	17	APE	airline
koonaa	17	APE	corner
koonetsu	26	SC	high fever
kootsuujiko	23	APE	auto accident
koshoo	22	APE	trouble
kossetsu	23	SC	bone fracture
kotae	25	APE	an answer
kotaeru	8	APE	to answer
kotoshi	16	SC	this year
kowagaru	5	APE	be afraid
kowai	26	SC	fearful, be afraid, scary
kowareru	16	APE	to break
kozutsumi	23	APE	package
kugatsu mikka	1	SC	September 3rd
kuji	10	SC	9 o'clock
kuni	19	SC	country
kuraku naru [*kurai*]	11	APE	to become dark
kusuri	7	APE	medicine
kuwashiku [*kuwashii*]	20	SC	in detail
kuyashii	23	APE	disappointed
kyanpu	14	APE	camping
kyanseru suru	25	APE	to cancel
kyookasho	7	APE	textbook
kyooryoku	28	SC	cooperation
kyooshi	11	APE	teacher
kyooshitsu	4	APE	classroom
kyoo wa zutto	14	APE	all day long
Kyuuba kiki	28	APE	Cuba crisis
kyuujitsu	29	APE	holiday
kyuu Yugo	28	APE	former Yugoslavia

(M)

maa	4	SC	well,....
maaku sareteru	22	SC	be marked
machi de	14	APE	on the street
mado	7	SC	window
madoguchi	17	APE	ticket window, counter
Maikeru Joodan	28	APE	Michael Jordan
mairu	26	APE	mile
Makudonarudo	19	APE	McDonald's
mane	14	APE	imitation
manga	11	APE	comic book
masshiro	14	APE	pure white
mata kondo	29	APE	some other time
Matsuda	23	APE	Mazda
matte [*matsu*]	29	SC	wait, just a moment
mattete [*matsu*]	7	APE	wait
mazeru	25	APE	to mix
mazu	26	SC	first, at first
meetoru	26	APE	meter
megami	8	SC	goddess
Meishiizu	19	APE	Macy's
Mekishiko	13	APE	Mexico
mensetsu o uke ni [*ukeru*]	5	APE	be interviewed
menzeiten	13	SC	duty-free shop
mezurashii	22	APE	rare, unusual
migi no	17	SC	on the right
mikake	14	APE	one's appearance
minami	19	SC	south
Minami Amerika	28	APE	South America
minami no	19	APE	southern
mi ni — [*miru*]	7	SC	... to see
minzoku	17	APE	race
mirarenai [*miru*]	8	SC	cannot see
miru	2	APE	to look
miseru	8	APE	to show
misete [*miseru*]	2	SC	let me see, show me
misoshiru	11	APE	miso soup
mitai [*miru*]	7	SC	want to see
mite [*miru*]	22	SC	look
mite morau [*miru*]	20	APE	to have [someone] see, to have [something] seen
miteta [*miru*]	7	SC	was looking

127

mo	25	APE	as many as, no less than
modoru	7	APE	to go back, to return
mono	11	SC	thing
moo	11	APE	already
moo chotto	29	APE	a little longer/more
moo...nai	7	APE	not ... anymore
morau	16	APE	to receive
motte iku [*motsu*]	20	APE	to bring
motte kuru [*motsu*]	7	SC	to bring, to carry
mukashi	19	APE	old times, long time ago
mukoo	23	APE	over there
muri	5	SC	over strain, overwork, force
muzukashii	16	SC	difficult
myuujishan	19	APE	musician

(N)

nagusameru	17	SC	to appease
naka	5	SC	inside
nakanaka	16	APE	hardly
nakayoku suru	28	APE	to get along with
nakihajimeta [*naku, hajimeru*]	26	SC	began to cry
naku	16	APE	to cry
nanbaa wan	28	APE	number one
Nan da.	2	SC	Oh boy!, What's the matter?
nandai	25	APE	how many [cars]
Nan da yo.	2	SC	What? What are you talking about?
nando	26	SC	how many degrees
Nani?	20	SC	What? Really?
nani ka	13	SC	anything
nani mo	5	APE	not ..... anything
Nani shiteta?	7	SC	What were you doing?
Nani yo.	2	SC	What?, Excuse me? Come on.
nanjikan	5	SC	how many hours
nannin	25	SC	how many people
naoru	20	APE	to get well
naraberu	8	APE	to arrange
narande susumu [*narabu*]	17	APE	to proceed in a line
natsu	1	SC	summer
natsukashiku [*natsukashii*]	1	SC	miss, long for, think fondly of
natsumatsuri	4	SC	summer festival
natsuyasumi	4	SC	summer vacation
nedan	25	APE	price

nedoko no yooi	17	APE	making a bed
neesan	2	SC	[one's own] elder sister
nekkuresu	14	APE	necklace
nemui	7	APE	sleepy
nemurenai [*nemuru*]	5	SC	cannot sleep
nemuru	5	SC	to sleep
nemusoo [*nemui*]	20	SC	look sleepy
nengajoo	16	SC	New Year's card
nenza	23	SC	sprain
neru	8	APE	to sleep
nesshin ni	20	SC	attentively
nete inai [*neru*]	20	SC	did not sleep
netsu	26	APE	fever
niau	2	SC	to suit, fit, complement, match/go well
nichiji	4	APE	the date and time
nigiru	16	APE	to grasp
nihonningyoo	13	SC	Japanese doll
nihonryokoo	28	SC	travel in/to Japan
nihonryoori	11	SC	Japanese food
nihonsei	19	SC	made in Japan
Nihon taiken	4	SC	experiences in Japan
nijukko	20	SC	twenty [boxes]
...ni naru	8	APE	to become ...
ningyoo	13	APE	doll
ninki	5	APE	popularity
nioi	11	SC	smell, scent
Nishi Doitsu	28	APE	West Germany
nittei	4	SC	schedule, program
nodo	5	APE	throat
nodo ga kawaku	22	APE	be thirsty
nokku suru	23	APE	to knock
nokoru	19	APE	to remain
nokotte [*nokoru*]	29	SC	remain
nomimono	4	APE	beverages
nomu	2	APE	to drink
norimashita [*noru*]	4	SC	took, went by, rode
noru	5	SC	to go by, to ride, to get on
noseru	16	APE	to give a ride, to give a lift
no yoo na	28	APE	such as, like
nyuugakushiken	4	APE	entrance examination
nyuugakushiki	4	APE	entrance ceremony
nyuuin	5	APE	hospitalization
nyuusu	13	APE	news

(O)

obaasan	13	APE	grandmother
obake	13	APE	ghost
oboeru	8	APE	to remember, to memorize
oboete imasu [*oboeru*]	11	SC	remember
Odaiji ni.	29	APE	Take care of yourself.
odoru	5	APE	to dance
ohakamairi	17	SC	a visit to a grave
ohanashi	4	SC	story; about...., on....
Ohisashiburi desu.	1	APE	It's been a long time
oisha san	20	APE	doctor
oishii	16	APE	taste good, delicious
ojiisan/ojiichan	20	APE	grandfather
Okaeri(nasai).	5	APE	Welcome home.
okashi	4	APE	Japanese sweets, candy
okiru	8	APE	to get up
okonomiyaki	23	APE	a pancake-like pizza
okoru	28	APE	to happen
okotte iru	22	APE	be angry
okuresoo [*okureru*]	14	APE	seem to be late
okutte [*okuru*]	2	SC	sent/send
okutte [*okuru*]	22	SC	give
okutta [*okuru*]	20	SC	sent
omairi	17	SC	a visit to a temple or shrine to pray
omamori	13	SC	charm
omatsuri	4	SC	festival
omiyage	2	SC	souvenir, gift
omoimashita [*omou*]	4	SC	thought
omotta [*omou*]	26	SC	thought
omou	25	SC	to think
onaka ga suku	22	APE	be hungry
ondo	26	APE	temperature
oneesan	13	SC	elder sister
oniisan	11	SC	elder brother
onna rashii	14	APE	typical of a woman
onsu	26	APE	ounce
ooame	23	APE	heavy rain
ooi	7	SC	many, large number of
ookikute [*ookii*]	8	SC	big and ...
Oranda	28	APE	Holland, the Netherlands
orenji juusu	19	APE	orange juice
orinpikku	28	SC	Olympics

oru	23	APE	to break
osara	20	APE	plates, dishes
Oseania	28	APE	Oceania
osewa	1	SC	hospitality, care, help, kindness
Osewa ni narimashita.	1	APE	Thank you very much for taking care of me.
oshiete [*oshieru*]	20	SC	explain, tell
oshoogatsu	17	SC	New Year's Day
osokatta [*osoi*]	7	SC	was late
Osuwari kudasai.	17	APE	Please have a seat.
otagai	28	APE	one another
oto	23	APE	sound
otoko rashii	14	APE	manly, macho
otona	1	APE	adult
otoshichatta [*otosu*]	20	APE	dropped
otosu	16	APE	to drop
ototoshi	13	APE	the year before last
otte iru [*oru*]	23	SC	broken
owarimasu [*owaru*]	1	SC	end, be over
owatta [*owaru*]	28	SC	ended, was over
oyashirazu o nuku	7	APE	to get one's wisdom teeth pulled out
Oyasumi kudasai.	17	APE	Sleep well.
oyu	25	APE	hot water

(P)

paatii	4	APE	party
pedaru	16	APE	pedal
penki o nuru	8	APE	to paint
penparu	4	SC	pen pal
pikunikku	20	APE	picnic
pitchaa	19	APE	pitcher [baseball]
pittari	2	SC	exactly, suitable, fit
pondo	26	APE	pound
Poorando	28	APE	Poland
poppusu	4	APE	pop music
puro futtobooru	11	APE	professional football

(R)

raishuu	25	SC	next week
raito	25	APE	light
rajikase	25	APE	radio cassette player
rashii	14	APE	I heard that ...
refurii	23	SC	referee

rei	17	SC	spirit
reisenjidai	28	SC	Cold War Period
rekishi	17	APE	history
renshuu	22	SC	practice, exercise, training
renshuu suru	8	APE	to practice
rokku	4	APE	rock music
Roshia	8	APE	Russia
Ruumania	28	APE	Romania
ryokoo	13	SC	trip, travel
ryokoo suru	5	APE	to travel
ryuugakusei	14	APE	foreign student
ryuugaku suru	2	APE	to study abroad

(S)

saafin	14	APE	surfing
Sadamu Fusein	28	APE	Saddam Hussein
saifu	20	APE	wallet
sagaru	26	APE	to go down
sagaseba [*sagasu*]	13	SC	if [one] looks for
saigo	11	SC	last
saikin	19	APE	recently
saikoo	10	APE	highest, high
saikoo	19	APE	excellent, best
saikuringu	16	APE	cycling
saitei	10	APE	lowest, low
sakki	16	APE	a while ago
sakura	19	APE	cherry blossom
sanka	28	SC	participation
sanka suru	28	SC	to participate
sanshin	28	APE	strikeout
sanshuukan	4	SC	three weeks
saraishuu	20	APE	the week after next
saru	16	SC	monkey
sarudoshi	16	SC	the year of the monkey
sashimi	7	APE	sliced raw fish
satoo	25	APE	sugar
se	8	APE	height
seetaa	14	APE	sweater
seien	22	SC	encouragement, support, cheer
seiji	28	APE	politics
seiki	8	APE	century
seinoo	14	SC	performance, quality

sekai	8	SC	the world
senchi	14	APE	centimeter
senchimeetoru	26	APE	centimeter
sensoo	28	APE	war
senshu	23	SC	player
senshu kootai	23	SC	player change
sensu	2	SC	Japanese folding fan
sentaku	11	APE	laundry
sentaku suru	16	APE	to do laundry
sesshi	26	SC	Celsius, Centigrade
shashin	1	SC	pictures, photos
shiai	22	SC	game
shiawase	5	APE	happiness
Shiazu Tawaa	8	APE	Sears Tower
shichiji	10	SC	7 o'clock
shigoto	11	APE	work, job
shika	25	APE	only
shiken	19	APE	examination
shikenbenkyoo	29	SC	study for an exam
shikkari	5	SC	well
shimaru	20	APE	be closed
shimatta	7	SC	darn
shimekiri	25	SC	deadline, closing
shimeru	8	APE	to close
shinamono	14	APE	merchandise
shinbun kiji	16	APE	newspaper article
shinchoo	25	APE	height
shinema	19	APE	cinema, movie theater
shinkansen	4	SC	bullet train
shinpai	23	SC	worry, concern, anxiety
shinpaisoo na kao o shite	26	SC	have a worried look on one's face
shinu	26	SC	to die
shiraberu	29	APE	to check, look into
shirabete [shiraberu]	16	SC	check
shiranakatta [shiru]	26	SC	didn't know
shiraseru	8	APE	to inform
shitai [suru]	8	APE	want to [do]
shitte iru [shiru]	2	SC	know
shitteta [shiru]	13	SC	knew
shizen	17	SC	natural
shokuji	14	APE	meal, food
shoogi	2	APE	chess

shoorai	17	APE	future
shoosan	22	APE	admiration
shootai suru	1	APE	to invite
shooyu	25	APE	soy sauce
shurui	25	APE	kind, sort
shuppatsu	17	APE	departure
shuppatsu suru	17	APE	to depart
shussekisha	4	APE	participants
shutchoo	20	APE	business trip
....shuu	4	APE	state
shuugakuryokoo	4	APE	school excursion
shuukyoo	19	SC	religion
shuuto	22	SC	shoot [basketball]
son	25	SC	loss, disadvantage
Soo ja nai.	20	SC	That's not right.; No, it isn't.
sooji suru	16	APE	to clean
Soo kanaa.	23	APE	Is that so?
soo suru to	26	APE	then
sorekara	5	APE	then
Soren	28	APE	former Soviet Union
soryaa	14	SC	of course
sosen	17	SC	ancestor
soshite	13	APE	then
soto	7	SC	outside
sotsugyoosei	1	APE	a graduate
sotsugyooshiki	4	APE	graduation ceremony
sugoi	22	SC	great, amazing
sugu	16	APE	immediately
sukaafu	13	APE	scarf
sukaato	14	APE	skirt
sukikirai	11	SC	particular, picky
sukunai	25	SC	few
sukunaku tomo	17	APE	at least
sumire	19	APE	violet
Supein	19	APE	Spain
Supuraito	19	APE	Sprite
suru hoo ga ii	7	APE	would be better to
sutairu	14	APE	style, one's figure
suteki	7	APE	cool, neat
suteru	25	APE	to throw away
suugaku	29	SC	mathematics

(T)

tabemono	4	APE	food
taberarenai [*taberu*]	11	SC	cannot eat
tabi	5	SC	trip
Tadaima.	5	APE	I'm home.
taifuu	25	APE	typhoon
taiikukan	2	APE	gymnasium
taikutsu	7	APE	bored
taion	26	APE	temperature
taionkei	26	SC	thermometer [body]
Taiwan	19	SC	Taiwan
takkyuubin	14	APE	a package delivery service
tako o ageru	22	APE	to fly a kite
tame ni	17	SC	for the purpose of, in order to
tana	16	APE	shelf
tanka	23	SC	stretcher
tanomu	14	APE	to ask a favor
tanoshikatta [*tanoshimu*]	4	SC	was fun, was enjoyable, enjoyed
tanoshimi	14	APE	pleasure, delight, be looking forward to
tanpopo	19	APE	dandelion
tashika	8	SC	be sure, surely
tasukaru	16	APE	be helpful
tatta	25	SC	only, small amount
tawaa	4	APE	tower
tazuneru	22	APE	to visit
tegami	1	SC	letter
tegowai	22	SC	tough
-te mo ii?	29	APE	May I ....?
tenkiyohoo	10	SC	weather forecast
te o furu	22	APE	to wave
te o futte iru [*furu*]	22	SC	waving
tera	17	SC	temple
terebi bangumi	19	APE	TV program
Tetsudatte kureru? [*tetsudau*]	7	APE	Could you help me?
tetsuya	20	APE	[stay up] all night
tobu	5	APE	to fly
todokeru	14	APE	to deliver
todoku	16	APE	to reach
tokehajimeru [*tokeru*]	11	APE	to start melting
toki	1	SC	time, when, while
tokidoki	2	SC	sometimes, occasionally
tokoro	10	SC	place
tokorode	29	SC	by the way

tokushuu	19	APE	special edition
tonari	20	APE	next, next door
tonikaku	5	SC	anyway
too	4	APE	ten
toochaku	17	APE	arrival
toochaku suru	17	APE	to arrive
toonan	19	SC	southeast
tootoo	4	SC	finally
tori ni — [*toru*]	7	SC	... to take, ... to get
toshi	17	SC	year
totemo .... dekinai [*dekiru*]	14	APE	could never do
tsuchi	11	APE	soil
tsugi	4	SC	next
tsuide	8	SC	at the same time
tsukaisute	7	SC	disposable
tsukamaru	13	APE	be caught
tsukaoo [*tsukau*]	2	SC	will use, will bring...to
tsukareru	7	APE	be tired
tsukeru	7	APE	to turn on
tsukiyubi o suru	23	APE	to sprain one's finger
tsukurikata [*tsukuru*]	19	APE	way of making, how to make
tsukuru	8	APE	to make
tsuri	7	APE	fishing
tsutaeru	13	APE	to tell, to inform
tsuushinhanbai	25	APE	mail-order
tsuyoi	14	APE	strong
tsuzukemasu [*tsuzukeru*]	23	SC	continue

(U)

uchi	29	SC	house
uchi no	20	APE	my, our
udon	20	APE	Japanese noodles
ugoku	5	APE	to move
umai	22	SC	good at, great
umi	14	APE	sea
undoo	5	APE	exercises
undookai	4	APE	sports festival, competition
unten menkyoshoo	16	APE	driver's license
unten suru	14	APE	to drive
uookuman	14	APE	walkman
ureshii	2	SC	be glad, be happy

(W)

wakaranai [*wakaru*]	29	SC	do not understand
Wangan	28	APE	the Persian Gulf

waru	26	SC	to divide
Warui kedo ...	29	APE	I'm sorry, but ....
wasurechatta [*wasureru*]	7	SC	forgot
wasurenai [*wasureru*]	25	SC	do not forget
wasurete imashita [*wasureru*]	13	SC	forgot

(Y)

yaku	25	APE	to bake
yaku	26	SC	about
yakusoku	2	APE	a promise, appointment
yamakaji	14	APE	forest fire
yappari	7	SC	as expected
yaru	5	APE	to do
yasai	19	APE	vegetables
yasashii	14	APE	soft, kind
yasuku [*yasui*]	10	APE	cheaply
yasumi	25	SC	day off, holiday, vacation
yatai	7	SC	food or game stand
yatsura	14	APE	guys
yatte kita [*yaru, kuru*]	23	SC	arrived, came
yatte miru	7	APE	to try
yattsukeru	14	APE	to beat
yokozuna	17	APE	sumo grand champion
yoku	5	APE	well
yonaka	20	SC	middle of the night
yoo	29	APE	errand
yoofuku	25	APE	clothes
...yoo ni.	17	APE	May ... be ...!; I wish ...
Yooroppa	19	APE	Europe
yoru	10	SC	night, nighttime
yosan	4	APE	budget
yoyaku	7	APE	reservation
yukata	4	SC	Japanese summer kimono
yuki	11	APE	snow

(Z)

zannen	23	SC	unfortunate, regrettable, too bad, a shame
zannen gatteru	23	SC	feel/be regretful, disappointed, sorry
zehi	14	APE	certainly
zenbu	28	SC	entire, all, whole
zen'in	4	APE	all members, everyone
zenzen ... nai	14	APE	not ... at all
zenzen chigau	23	APE	totally different
zettai (ni)	8	SC	absolutely, definitely
zuibun	1	SC	very much, extremely